THE REGENCY
COUNTRY HOUSE

THE REGENCY COUNTRY HOUSE

FROM THE ARCHIVES OF COUNTRY LIFE

JOHN MARTIN ROBINSON

AURUM PRESS

First published in Great Britain 2005 by Aurum Press Limited
25 Bedford Avenue, London WC1B 3AT
www.aurumpress.co.uk

Design by James Campus
Originated, printed and bound in Singapore by CS Graphics

Frontispiece: *The library at Arundel Castle, Sussex, designed by the 11th Duke of Norfolk in 1800.*
Front endpaper: *Luscombe Castle, Devon.*
Rear endpaper: *The Sculpture Gallery, Woburn Abbey, Bedfordshire.*

THE COUNTRY LIFE PICTURE LIBRARY

The *Country Life* Picture Library holds a complete set of prints made from its
negatives, and a card index to the subjects, usually recording the name of the photographer and the date of the photographs catalogued, together with a separate index of
photographers. It also holds a complete set of *Country Life* and various forms of
published indices to the magazine. The Library may be visited by appointment, and
prints of any negatives it holds can be supplied by post.

For further information, please contact the Librarian, Camilla Costello, at *Country
Life*, King's Reach Tower, Stamford Street, London SE1 9LS (*Tel:* 020 7261 6337).

ACKNOWLEDGEMENTS

I would like to thank the splendid 'home team': Camilla Costello of the *Country Life*
Picture Library, Jeremy Musson, the architectural editor, whose idea this book was,
James Campus, the designer, Margaret Lancaster, who transferred my script from ink
to computer, and, not least, Clare Howell, the book's stalwart editor.

LIST OF ARTICLES

This is a list of *Country Life* articles for which the photographs reproduced in this
book were taken. The photographer's name is given (in brackets) if known.

Angeston Grange, Gloucestershire: 1 March 2001 (Paul Barker).

Arundel Castle, Sussex: 23 April 1998 (June Buck).

Ashridge Park, Hertfordshire: 6 August 1921 (Ward); 13 August 1921.

Barnsley Park, Gloucestershire: 2 and 9 September 1954 (A. E. Henson).

The Beach House, Sussex: 29 January 1921 (Sleigh).

Belsay Hall, Northumberland: 5 and 12 October 1940 (A. E. Henson); 13 September
1990; 5 September 1996.

Belvoir Castle, Leicestershire: 6, 13, 20 and 27 December 1956 (A. E. Henson);
23 June 1994 (Paul Barker).

Bignor Park, Sussex: 3 May 1956 (Gunn).

Brighton Pavilion: *Country Life* Annual 1964 (Alex Starkey).

Broughton Hall, Yorkshire: 7 April 1950 (A. E. Henson).

Buckingham Palace, London: 14 February 1931 (A. E. Henson and Gill).

Chatsworth, Derbyshire: 5, 12, 19 and 26 January 1918; 11, 18 and 25 April 1968
(Alex Starkey); 7 April 1994 (Tim Imrie-Tait).

Chillington Hall, Staffordshire: 13, 20 and 27 February 1948 (A. E. Henson);
10 September 1953; 30 September 1999 (Paul Barker).

Cranbury Park, Hampshire: 25 October 1956 (Gunn); 8 and 15 November 1956
(Gunn).

Cronkhill, Shropshire: 19 February 2004 (Alex Ramsay).

Deene Park, Northamptonshire: 18 April 1976 (Alex Starkey).

The Deepdene, Surrey: 20 May 1899 (Charles Latham).

Eastnor Castle, Herefordshire: 14 March 1968 (J. Gibson); 13 May 1993
(Tim Imrie-Tait).

Eaton Hall, Cheshire: 11 and 18 February 1971 (Alex Starkey).

Endsleigh Cottage, Devon: 9 October 1997 (Tim Imrie-Tait).

Gillow furniture: 15 June 1978 (Alex Starkey).

Goodwood Park, Sussex: 25 September 1997 (Tim Imrie-Tait); 23 April 1998
(Tim Imrie-Tait).

Houghton Lodge, Hampshire: 7, 20 and 27 April 1951 (Westley).

Ickworth Park, Suffolk: 31 October and 25 November 1925 (A. E. Henson);
10 March 1955 (J. Gibson); 8 March 1956.

Luscombe Castle, Devon: 9, 16 and 23 February 1956 (Gunn).

Meldon Park, Northumberland: 14 April 1950; 24 February 1966.

Moggerhanger, Bedfordshire: 2005 (June Buck).

Oakly Park, Shropshire: 22 March 1990 (Tim Imrie-Tait).

Panshanger Hall, Hertfordshire: 11 and 18 January 1936 (A. E. Henson).

Penrhyn Castle, Gwynedd (Caernarvonshire): 5 November 1987 (Mark Fiennes).

Pitzhanger Manor, Ealing: 22 February 1919; 10 September 1953; 2 September 1999
(Paul Barker).

Port Eliot, Cornwall: 15, 22 and 29 October 1948 (Westley).

Sezincote, Gloucestershire: 13 and 20 May 1939 (A. E. Henson); 2 September 1976
(J. Gibson); 10 January 2002 (Melanie Eclare).

Sheringham Hall, Norfolk: 31 January 1957 (A. E. Henson); 7 February 1957
(A. E. Henson).

Southill, Bedfordshire: 12 July 1930 (Gill and A. E. Henson); 19 and 26 July 1930;
23 March 1951; 28 April 1994 (Julian Nieman).

Stratfield Saye, Hampshire: 10 April 1975 (Alex Starkey).

Tatton Park, Cheshire: 16 and 23 July 1964 (Alex Starkey).

Tregothnan, Cornwall: 17 and 24 May 1956.

Willey Park, Shropshire: 19 February 1921.

Windsor Castle, Berkshire: *Country Life* Annual 1952 (Alex Starkey).

Woburn Abbey, Bedfordshire: 1949 (Westley).

Wotton House, Buckinghamshire: 13 May 2004 (Paul Barker).

Wynyard Park, County Durham: 1 September 1988 (Julian Nieman).

CONTENTS

*

THE English country house as we know it – the centre of a self-contained estate and the setting for house parties – is essentially a product of the Regency era. Many of its distinctive characteristics were established in the thirty or forty years from the 1790s to 1830, between the first 'madness' of George III and the death of George IV. These are the dates loosely but conventionally considered to be 'Regency', rather than the strict calendar of the constitutional Regency from 1811 to 1820, and the term refers to an English style in architecture and decoration contemporaneous with Empire in France.

The Regency saw the flowering of the Picturesque as the defining English aesthetic. The British landscape came to be admired in the early nineteenth century, pre-eminently for its natural beauty, seen as the finest north of the Alps. It was extolled by poets, and celebrated by great artists, such as Constable, Turner, Daniells, Ward, Loutherberg, and most of the English School of Watercolour. Thus, the countryside and country house life were admired and enjoyed for their own sake – as they are today – though houses were also still regarded as political power bases. The latter role, however, was beginning to change, a process acknowledged by the Great Reform Bill, finally passed in 1832, two years after the death of George IV, which tipped the balance of political representation from the country to the towns. The English country house and its way of life in the early 1800s was a model admired and imitated throughout Europe and even Russia.

The Regency period saw the culmination of the eighteenth-century improvements in agriculture and estate management which we call the 'Agricultural Revolution'. Prior to the eighteenth century, great estates had been sprawling agglomerations of mixed lands, feudal dues, and customary rights and tenures, being as much legal concepts as physical entities. By the early nineteenth century, most English estates had become ring-fenced units with self-contained tenant farms, villages of model cottages, and centralised management by a new breed of professional land agent. Outlying properties had been sold, customary tenancies and anachronistic manorial rights bought out or enfranchised, the farms re-organised and woods planted to create the recognisable modern rural landscape.

Landowners often used investment income from elsewhere, as well as enclosure of the land, to consolidate their home estates. Enclosure of previously open land had proceeded since the sixteenth century, with open fields and commons being divided into separate hedged farms. The process was speeded up at the end of the eighteenth century by a general enabling Act of Parliament. The boundaries and physical characteristics of many of the estates around the great English houses still survive as created at this time, including Chatsworth, Arundel, Belvoir, Eaton and Woburn.

In Cheshire, where formerly there had been fourteen proprietors around Eaton Hall, by 1811, as now, there was just the Grosvenor family. At Woburn, the trustees of the 5th Duke of Bedford (who died in 1802) bought out all the surrounding landowners; at Arundel, between 1790 and the 1830s, the 11th and 12th Dukes of Norfolk used money from sales in Sheffield to double the size of the estate; Coke of Norfolk (later created 1st Earl of Leicester) at Holkham Hall disposed of all his properties in Oxfordshire and Lancashire to enlarge and consolidate his Norfolk holdings.

So, by the early nineteenth century, hardly anything remained of the medieval landscape of peasants, open fields, manorial dues, or even of Tudor yeomen. Much of the lowland Regency countryside is recognisable today with intensive, scientific farming combined with consciously beautiful amenity planting, sporting coverts, and artistically contrived landscape improvements.

New houses were carefully sited to take advantage of the views, rather than for shelter or other more utilitarian reasons. The architecture of the Regency house, and the design of the surrounding park and estate, were developed as carefully related harmonies. Sometimes the dramatic, romantic architecture created a focus and crown for the landscape, as at Belvoir Castle, but more often the austerity of the house served as a counterfoil to lush planting, as at Belsay Hall, Bignor Park, or Meldon Park. Much of this landscape work and the care put into siting houses drew on the advice of Payne Knight and Uvedale Price, whose influential writings on the Picturesque had been published in the 1790s. Much of the actual landscaping was done by Humphry Repton, who was ubiquitous, or at least his style was, made popular through a series of publications illustrated with views of the landscape 'before' and 'after', using movable flaps superimposed on the original scene to display the garden in maturity.

Long entrance drives, in particular, were contrived through the surrounding (owned) country to build up a dramatic sense of anticipation. That at Tregothnan in Cornwall meanders for 3 miles, with dramatic views of the sea and estuary alternating with thick, impervious plantations. At Eaton Hall in Cheshire, exaggerated approaches from the different points of the compass crossed over ordinary roads and even the River Dee on bridges, and linked the house at the centre of the

EASTNOR CASTLE, HEREFORDSHIRE Above: *Early-nineteenth-century watercolour of the dining room. The plain Gothic architecture of this room relied on strong colours for its impact. The Gothic, tripartite, arcaded alcove for a massive built-in sideboard is a typical Regency feature.*

CHATSWORTH, DERBYSHIRE Left: *The Great Dining Room designed by Jeffry Wyatville.*

newly enlarged estate to the surrounding picturesque villages – an effect made more astonishing later in the nineteenth century by the lavish fruits of Victorian philanthropy. Pride of ownership mingled happily with aesthetic pleasure.

Harriet, Countess Granville, describing the grounds of her husband's family seat at Trentham in Staffordshire in 1828, captures well the Regency view of the countryside: 'This is in many ways a beautiful place and the *tenue*, the neatness, the training of flowers and fruit trees, gates, enclosures, hedges are what in no other country is dreamt of; and there is repose, a *laisser aller*, a freedom, and a security in a *vie de château* that no other offers one. I feel when I set out to walk as if alone in the world – nothing but trees and birds; but then comes the enormous satisfaction of always finding a man dressing a hedge, or a woman in gingham and a black bonnet on her knees picking up weeds, the natural gendarmerie of the country, and most comfortable well-organised country.'

The landed estate provided the setting and part of the economic base for the Regency country house. Agriculture was lucrative in the late Georgian period. The first half of the Regency coincided with the Napoleonic Wars and blockades of trade and imports. The need to feed a rapidly expanding urban population from home produce created high profits for landowners and farmers alike. The regular income of English landowners, both great and small, in those years was, however, only part agricultural. Then, as now, the money that supported thriving country houses came from elsewhere. The riches of the English upper classes, which so amazed foreign visitors and commentators, derived from rapid industrialisation, the exploitation of minerals and building development, as well as investments, overseas trade and banking.

It was the money from these capitalist sources that paid for many of the houses illustrated in this book, just as it does for new houses built today. Ashridge in Hertfordshire was entirely created out of the proceeds of the Bridgewater Canal fortune (made in Manchester). The princely aggrandisement of Chatsworth in the 1820s was possible because of vast mineral royalties, including the copper mine at Ecton in Staffordshire, and urban development at the new spa town of Buxton

(and, indeed, by capital sales such as the Londesborough estate in the East Riding). At Eaton Hall in Cheshire, the Grosvenor fortune was based on London ground rents, as well as on mining revenue from Wales; the Norfolks' fortune, which reconstructed Arundel Castle in Sussex, came from canal wharfs, markets, coal, iron and ground rents in Sheffield, cotton at Glossop, some London ground rents, and urban development at Littlehampton; the Bedfords – then the richest of the lot – had extensive urban ground rents in Bloomsbury, the Covent Garden markets, and mining in Devon and Cornwall.

Penrhyn Castle in North Wales was a gigantic celebration of the success of the Bethesda Slate Quarry, itself fuelled by Liverpool–West Indies income; Eastnor Castle, Herefordshire, was financed by the development of Somers Town in London; Sezincote in Gloucestershire was the creation of an East India Company fortune; Oakly Park, Shropshire, a combination of Indian nabobry and Cardiff ground rents; Meldon Park, Northumberland, was the newly established seat of a Newcastle coal owner; Thomas Hope's Deepdene, of course, was entirely the produce of banking, as were the Barings' various Hampshire houses so hated by William Cobbett, who contrasted their frigid Grecian symmetries and plantations of fir trees with an imagined rural past of pink-cheeked, yeoman happiness. The Regency country house was the product of the world's first modern economy.

'The "nimbus" of a firmly anchored aristocracy and vast wealth (combined with admirable taste in spending it …) has stamped the Great World of this country as that *par excellence* of Europe,' wrote Prince Pückler-Muskau in 1826. Envious Germans and French consoled themselves with the thought that while the English upper class was astonishingly rich, it was not by their standards very noble, being in only a few cases the male line descendant of a medieval peerage. Prince Pückler-Muskau in his delightfully perspicacious journals of visits to England in 1815 and 1826–27 understood this and it is worth

CARLTON HOUSE, LONDON Above left: *The porte-cochère on the entrance front designed by Henry Holland for the Prince Regent.*

ALTON TOWERS, STAFFORDSHIRE Above: *Developed by successive architects in the early nineteenth century for the earls of Shrewsbury.*

WOBURN ABBEY, BEDFORDSHIRE *The sculpture gallery opened by Jeffry Wyatville within Henry Holland's greenhouse.*

quoting him: 'The English nobility, haughty as it is, can scarcely measure itself against the French in antiquity and purity of blood … It dazzles only by the old historic names, so wisely retained, which appear through the whole of English history like standing masks; though new families, often of very mean and even discreditable extraction … are continually concealed behind them. The English aristocracy has indeed the most solid advantages over those of all other countries – from its real wealth, and yet more from the share in the legislative power allotted to it by the constitution.'

He was, no doubt, thinking of his old friend the Earl of Darnley – magnificently seated at Tudor Cobham in a Repton landscape in Kent – whose great-grandfather was an Irish grazier called Bligh; or of the 3rd Duke of Northumberland, whose grandfather had changed his name to Percy from Smithson and was descended from a London draper; or Lord Holland, whose great-grandfather had been a footman. The Osbornes, dukes of Leeds, were descended from clothworkers, the Earl of Radnor from 'an eminent Turkey merchant of the City of London', the Earl of Craven from a tailor. The families of Dartmouth, Ducie, Pomfret, Tankerville, Dormer, Romney, Dudley, Fitzwilliam, Cowper, Leigh, Hill and Normanby 'all sprang from London shops and counting houses and that not so very long ago,' as Price Collier acidly noted.

The English Regency aristocracy was, like that of the Republic of Venice, largely mercantile in origin, but smothered itself in neo-feudal trappings and Norman-sounding suffixes in order to seem more 'blue blooded'. An amusing social footnote of the late eighteenth and early nineteenth centuries in Britain was the Gothicising of ordinary English names by Royal Licence. Mr Green became de Freville, Mr Wilkins, de Winton, Mr Hunt, de Vere, Mr Morres, de Montmorency. Resounding new peerages also often disguised a more humdrum nomenclature. Lord Carrington was Mr Smith, the banker; Lord de Montalt, Mr Maude; Lord de Freyne, Mr French; Lord de Dunstanville, Mr Basset. The owners of such borrowed 'medieval' plumage usually favoured Gothic for their houses. So did genuinely old families like the Talbots, earls of Shrewsbury, who created a Regency Gothic wonderland at Alton Towers in Staffordshire, redolent as Pevsner noted 'of the highest dreams of Catholic Romanticism'.

STRATFIELD SAYE, HAMPSHIRE Above: *The prints on the wall, the Boulle furniture and the Colza chandeliers reflect the taste of the 1st Duke of Wellington.*

Left: *The library as refurnished in Regency taste, and enhanced in 1947.*

Pückler-Muskau understood that the driving force in Regency society was not blood, or even wealth and power, but fashion or *ton* in contemporary parlance – celebrity in ours. Fashion in England was the 'supreme and absolute sovereign'. In the eighteenth century under the Hanoverian monarchs, fashion had been dictated by the rich aristocracy, beneficiaries of the 1688 Revolution, because there was no British Court in the Continental sense. 'The Kings of England live like private men; most of the high officers about the Court are little more than nominal, and are seldom assembled except on occasions of great ceremony', like the Coronation or State Opening of Parliament. Pückler-Muskau noted that George III was not a man of fashion, but that his son, the Prince Regent, definitely was, a personal rather a royal attribute.

In Regency society, the Prince was the ultimate *arbiter elegantiorum*, and that was unparalleled in recent English history. He pioneered several of the defining characteristics of the Regency country house, not just architectural fashions and decorative styles, but many of the social innovations and new forms of entertaining which had a lasting impact on country house life. The Prince and his circle were responsible for adopting the later hour for fashionable dining between 6 and 7 p.m. rather than 3 in the afternoon; for the gradual change from *service à la française* to *service à la russe* with dishes handed round by footmen rather than all placed on the table at once, even for the form of the classic silver dinner service as evolved in these years under the Prince's extravagant patronage by the Crown goldsmith, Rundell, Bridge and Rundell, and the invention of specialist bits of cutlery, such as asparagus tongs and fish slices.

The Prince also set a lead in technical innovations in the domestic sphere, not least central heating, oil and gas lighting, and novel kitchen gadgetry. He provided comfortable bedrooms where guests could stay for days or even weeks at a time at Brighton or Windsor, thus inventing the modern house party. He made the country house visiting season from late autumn to spring fashionable by descending for long visits at the houses of favoured cronies (lavishly done up for the occasion) like Ragley (the Marquess of Hertford), Uppark (Sir Harry Fetherstonhaugh), Renishaw (Sir Sitwell Sitwell), Hinchingbrooke (the Earl of Sandwich), and Belvoir (the Duke of Rutland).

In reaction to his spartan upbringing and as a young man with no political or military role, the Prince found an outlet for his aspirations in the visual arts. He pursued these throughout his life, in the creation of a series of spectacular residences, and in eclectic, obsessive connoisseurship, regardless of expense. His decorating, collecting, architectural patronage, and landscape gardening were compulsive. They set the tone for the Regency style, beginning with the Francophile elegance of Henry Holland's Carlton House and Brighton Pavilion (Mark I), then the astonishing Orientalising of Brighton Pavilion (Mark II), which single-handedly revived the taste for chinoiserie, then Royal Lodge at Windsor, which set the seal on the fashion for 'cottage

residences', and finally, Windsor Castle and Buckingham Palace, the grandest residences of the period (the first greatly admired, the latter not).

The Prince's frequent redecorating schemes at Carlton House and Brighton were in the vanguard and established many of the stylistic fashions of the period, notably the dominating role of upholstery with swagged and tasselled curtains, military tent rooms, and thick-pile fitted carpets; glass or ormolu chandeliers as big as houses – 'rooms as full of lamps as Hancock's shop', in Crocker's phrase; heavy over-gilding and astonishingly bright colours: crimson lake, chrome yellow, emerald green, Garter blue, peach, pink and purple. He inspired the vogue for stained glass in domestic interiors, *ancien régime* French furniture and Sèvres porcelain, and ornate gold plate – gilt silver had been comparatively rare in eighteenth-century England. He also helped create a taste for 'opulence … and barbaric splendour' which filtered down from perfumed and over-heated royal rooms to the country seats of squires, industrialists and bankers, partly through pattern books such as the *Cabinet-makers' and Upholsterers' Drawing Book* – a compendium of pelmets and curtains by George Smith, 'upholder to the Prince Regent'.

Houses were built or remodelled and extended in the Regency period to accommodate a more developed social life with rooms designed for specific functions and activities – breakfast rooms, billiard rooms, sculpture galleries, picture galleries, ballrooms – often opening up in continuous axial enfilades, with doors arranged in a straight line. This marked a radical departure from Georgian planning which, as late as the 1760s and 1770s, still perpetuated the Baroque idea of the state apartment, even in architecturally progressive houses like Adam's Osterley, Kedleston and Harewood. The use of country houses now became more like London houses, geared up for entertaining smart guests in a metropolitan way, with rooms for cards, music, dancing and theatricals. When Lord Nelson visited Fonthill in 1801, William Beckford arranged a London-style entertainment after a spectacular dinner, with solemn music and Lady Hamilton performing her famous 'Attitudes' in the 'character of Agrippa bearing the Ashes of Germanicus in a golden urn'.

The *vie de château* in Regency houses is extremely well documented in the correspondence and journals of contemporaries – not only by foreigners like Pückler-Muskau, Princess Lieven and the duchesse de Dino (Talleyrand's niece), but also by indefatigable English diarists like Greville and Creevey, or brilliant letter-writers like Harriet Granville – all of whom have left a vivid picture of the Regency country house in action. In addition to which it has achieved immortality in fiction. The novels of Jane Austen give a crystalline and delightful picture of social life in smaller country houses, while Thackeray did the same for the smart set – dinners, balls, visits, and house parties, the authentic mix of the fashionable, relations and hangers-on. The larger Regency house was devised primarily for grand entertaining, rather than mere family life.

During the Regency, as Mark Girouard has explained in *Life in The English Country House* (1978), the range and type of country house parties were greatly extended. In previous eras, country house entertaining had been different from that in London. In the Middle Ages and under the Tudors, parties in country houses celebrated particular events such as the great feasts of the year or rent days, and included all ranks. In the eighteenth century, new entertainments had originated, including house-warmings and coming-of-age parties, estate hospitality for tenants, servants and employees, while field sports, especially hunting, provided a social bedrock in the country.

The eighteenth-century ball, however, with its emphasis on dancing cotillions and minuets, the house specially decorated, and a lavish supper afterwards, was a London invention attended only by upper class guests. In the late eighteenth and early nineteenth centuries, this and other metropolitan types of entertainment spread to the country house, with invited fashionable guests and a more equal mix of men and women. The early nineteenth century also saw advances in shooting with the development of more accurate and reliable guns, and the innovation of driven game with beaters, rather than 'walking up'.

SOUTHILL, BEDFORDSHIRE Above left: *The boudoir designed by Henry Holland.*

BARNSLEY PARK, GLOUCESTERSHIRE Right: *The library added by John Nash, 1807.*

This made possible larger-scale shooting parties in the modern manner. These first took place at Holkham in Norfolk under Coke of Norfolk and soon rapidly spread elsewhere.

The reign of George III had seen the whole of Britain interconnected by good toll roads with tarmacadam surfaces. These reached their zenith during the Regency age under the direction of Pitt's Board of Agriculture and the Post Office. Good, smooth roads and the British development and manufacture of all kinds of efficient, innovative and speedy new carriages – phaetons, curricles, broughams, chariots – as well as the public stagecoach made this the golden age of English road travel. An unremarked but significant detail of the carriage accident on Salisbury Plain in 1813, when James Wyatt was killed travelling back to London in Sir Christopher Codrington's coach from Gloucestershire, was that the architect was reading a newspaper at the time, although travelling at the high speed of 12 m.p.h. This is a striking testimony to the stability of the springs of the coach and the smoothness of the road.

An architectural reflection of improvements in vehicular travel was the development of the porte-cochère, a new architectural feature for wheeled arrival under cover which made its first appearance at Carlton House and was adopted by the Wyatts at Dodington, Willey,

Wynyard and Windsor, by Robert Smirke at Eastnor, Thomas Hopper at Penrhyn, Humphry Repton at Cobham, Sir John Thoroton at Belvoir, and William Wilkins at Tregothnan.

Good road communications made country houses much more accessible, even before the development of the railways in the 1830s and 1840s, and this boosted the popularity of the house party. In big Regency houses like Belvoir and Chatsworth, thirty or forty guests would stay at a time. The weekend, 'Saturday to Monday' party was a Regency invention in addition to the more established convention for longer parties. (Sir Robert Walpole, for instance, in the 1730s had had political supporters to stay at Houghton for six days or more, hunting and drinking). In the Regency period there emerged a specific country season from December to April, including Christmas and New Year, when guests came to stay and the house was *en fête*. This balanced the London seasons, in early summer and autumn. This type of entertaining dictated the character and planning of Regency country houses, and was responsible for their modern-seeming arrangements.

The novelty of the Regency house party was its relaxed informality and variety. Pückler-Muskau gives an idea in his description of a stay at Cobham with the Earl of Darnley in February 1827. 'After dinner I

observed the company was distributed in the following manner. Our suffering host [Lord Darnley was a martyr to gout] lay on the sofa, dozing a little; five ladies and gentlemen were very attentively reading … another had been playing for a quarter of an hour with a long-suffering dog; two old Members of Parliament were disputing vehemently about the "Corn Bill" … Light supper of cold meats and fruit. Everyone retires at 12. Servants already in bed.' He admitted that country house life was 'without question the most agreeable side of English life; for there is great freedom, and banishment of most of the wearisome ceremonies which, with us, tire both host and guests. Notwithstanding this, one finds not less luxury than in the town …'.

The painter Robert Haydon gives an equally attractive picture of a house party at Petworth as a guest of the Earl of Egremont in 1826. 'Dogs, horses, cows, deer and pigs, peasantry and servants, guests and family all share alike his bounty and opulence and luxuries. At breakfast, after the guests have breakfasted, in walks Lord Egremont; first comes a grandchild whom he sends away happy. Outside the window moan a dozen black spaniels, who are let in, and to them he distributes cakes and comfits, giving all equal shares. After chatting with one guest, and proposing some scheme of pleasure to others, his leather gaiters are buttoned on, and away he walks, leaving everybody to take care of themselves, with all that opulence and generosity can place at their disposal [including a studio for Turner to paint in] … At dinner he meets everybody … All principal dishes he helps … There is plenty, but not absurd profligacy, good wines, but not extravagant waste. Everything is solid, liberal, rich and English.'

The Regency house party was, as Girouard commented, the 'pleasantest way of passing time ever devised.' Breakfast was set out either in the dining room or the breakfast room – a new innovation – until the whole party had done, helping themselves from silver dishes on spirit-heated warmers (an invention of Matthew Boulton's in Birmingham) on the sideboard. At Newstead Abbey in 1806, Byron and his rakish friends never had breakfast before 11 a.m. At Woburn, breakfast lasted from 10 to 12 with individual little gold teapots. At Windsor, when George IV finally moved into his new apartments in 1829, the ladies had breakfast in their rooms and light luncheon was served at 2 p.m., another royal innovation.

The company in houses occupied themselves how they wished during the day: sport, sight-seeing, walking or riding in the miles of wood, park and gardens, conversation, reading, painting, writing, music, looking at prints, or indoor games like billiards or shuttlecock. An idea of the range of Regency daytime activities in a great house can be obtained at Woburn from the quarter-mile covered circuit from the south to the north ends of the house beyond the stable blocks, devised by the 5th and 6th Dukes of Bedford. It took in the sculpture gallery, a museum, hothouses full of orchids and cacti (acquired with the botanist Sir William Hooker's advice and given to Kew on the 6th Duke's death), the Real Tennis court, the riding school and, finally, the Chinese dairy with its Oriental porcelain, cream and butter.

Dinner was the great event, with everybody dressed as smartly as possible, the footmen in full livery, and the new Paul Storr silver dinner

services (every house must have had one or two), a blaze of candlelight (necessary because of the later dining hour) and an admixture of invited neighbours to leaven the house guests. Afterwards there was tea, music (several houses having their own bands or orchestra, as at Chatsworth or Belvoir), theatricals and general jollity. At Christmas at Hinchingbrooke when the Prince of Wales stayed, he played the violincello, and his host, Lord Sandwich, the kettledrums. Byron's friends at Newstead dressed up as monks and drank burgundy from human skulls after dinner.

More conventionally smart were the balls and theatre at Woburn and Chatsworth. The servants usually disappeared immediately after dinner (they had to get up early), leaving a cold supper (sandwiches at Newstead) for people to help themselves, and silver chamber candle-

BELVOIR CASTLE, LEICESTERSHIRE Top: *The King's Bedroom.*
STOURHEAD, WILTSHIRE Above: *The library, with furniture by Chippendale.*
Left: *Sir Richard Colt Hoare's picture gallery, photographed in the late nineteenth century.*

sticks in the hall for guests to light their way to bed. A respectable house party usually went to bed at 11 or 12 p.m., but Byron's went on until 2 or 3 in the morning.

The smartest Regency parties were probably those at Woburn, Belvoir and Chatsworth, where the grand Whiggery gathered every winter, intermixed with the cream of European diplomats, the Lievens, Esterhazys and Talleyrands; and the Duke of Wellington always came to shoot (not very well, Lord John Russell noted at Woburn). Harriet Granville wrote after staying with the Bedfords: 'We left Woburn yesterday, having spent there a week of as much pleasure as is compatible with seeing it end without regret, the *locale* itself is a great source of enjoyment. There is so much space, so much comfort, such *luxe* and ease. The society generally very good, much to amuse and nothing to annoy,' though she found it slightly tedious having 'to dress up very smart and sitting often at dinner between Lords Tavistock and Worcester'. That strikes an authentic note – the place wonderful, but the people ... Talleyrand agreed. '*Tenez c'est beau, on ne peut pas disputer le goût,*' he exclaimed, looking out of a window at Woburn towards the lakes and planting, which Repton had improved in 1806.

Lady Shelley in 1812 gives an amusing vignette of an evening at Woburn. 'As soon as we left the dining room, the Duchess went to her nursing employment [she had a baby daughter whom she was feeding herself] ... and we dispersed ... through an enfilade of six rooms. The gentlemen soon joined us and in the first Shelley got a companion for billiards. In the next Lady Asgill established herself in an attitude lying on the sofa with Sir Thomas Graham at her feet. In the next Lady Jane [Montagu] and Miss Russell at a harp and pianoforte (both out of tune) playing the Creation ... In the gallery a few pairs were dispersed on sofas ... Scarcely was I seated when the Duchess entered and collecting her romping force of girls and young men, they all seized cushions and began pelting the whist players.'

The practical logistics in organising all this were stupendous. Greville tells us that the Duke of Bedford employed over 400 people on the Woburn estate, and Sir Robert Peel thought that the ducal

GOODWOOD PARK, SUSSEX Above: *The Egyptian-style dining room designed by James Wyatt, with sienna scagliola walls.*

DEENE PARK, NORTHAMPTONSHIRE Right: *The library added to the Elizabethan house c. 1810 as one of a range of Regency reception rooms.*

workshops and outbuildings resembled a naval dockyard (then the largest industrial enterprises in England). Another insight into the statistics of Regency country house entertaining can be gleaned from the early-nineteenth-century steward's accounts at Belvoir for the winter season there when, between December and April (including Christmas), 1,997 people dined at the ducal table in the castle, 2,421 in the Steward's Room (upper servants) and 11,312 in the Servants' Hall, nursery and kitchen department, including outside callers. Two hundred dozen bottles of wine and 70 hogsheads of ale were drunk, 2,330 wax candles burnt, and 630 gallons of oil consumed in the lamps in four months.

Entertaining on this scale explains the size and purpose of the principal rooms in a great Regency house. But as Pückler-Muskau saw, this lavish hospitality was confined to the country season. For the rest of the year, the family lived quietly on their own, eating boiled mutton and rice pudding (another Regency invention, referred to by Jane Austen). The separation of private life and hospitality dictated an important aspect of Regency house planning, the provision of small family rooms for everyday living – a cosy little sitting room for the lady of the house and a 'business room' for the man where he could do his paperwork as a landowner, JP, or even scholar; day and night nurseries and a schoolroom for the children; and a general family living room.

At Sheringham Hall in Norfolk, the nest of a young married couple who did not wish to entertain much, the plan devised by Repton included a business room, a sitting room and a library-living room, but no drawing room at all. This kind of simplicity marks the other end of the scale from the smart social houses with their enfilades of six or seven entertaining rooms. Repton advocated 'one large living room to contain books, 'instruments, tables and everything requisite to modern comfort and costume …'.

The standard Regency country house contained three principal rooms: the library, the drawing room, and the dining room. The large library-living room was one of the great innovations of Regency domestic planning; it was the heart of most country houses, regardless of their scale. In the early eighteenth century, libraries were not usually one of the principal rooms but were remote sanctums, though from the 1730s at Kelmarsh, Kirtlington and in other instances, they had been one of the main living rooms. In the later eighteenth century, in the houses of Adam and Wyatt, for example, libraries had come to form part of the main enfilade, at Syon and Heveningham, for instance, and Henry Holland made the libraries at Althorp and Woburn the largest and most magnificent rooms in the house.

By the Regency period, the library was often not just the principal room, but was distinctively and comfortably furnished with a variety of tables for specific purposes – sofa tables, writing tables, reading tables, book stands, games tables, circular library tables. There was also a range of comfortably upholstered seat furniture – sofas, couches, armchairs, library chairs, ottomans – often informally arranged in free-standing groups in the middle of the room and around the fireplace, rather than placed formally along the walls as had been the practice earlier. The freestanding Grecian couch was a Regency invention and a very popular one to judge from contemporary descriptions of house parties where at least one of the guests was always to be found lolling on one after dinner. A comfortably furnished library-living room formed part of the plans for George IV's successive residences at Carlton House, Windsor Castle and Buckingham Palace, and at Arundel, Chatsworth, Belsay, Tatton and other Regency ensembles, the library was the largest and principal sitting room. Libraries were also contrived in or added on to older houses, as at Stourhead, Deene and Barnsley Park.

This emphasis on the library in the Regency house is also a reflection of the great age of English bibliomania. The 2nd Earl Spencer at Althorp and the 6th Duke of Devonshire at Chatsworth were the greatest book collectors of their time. The Roxburghe Club, the oldest bibliophile society in the world, was founded in 1812, with Lord Spencer as president. The Regency saw English book production reach its greatest heights with beautiful type by Baskerville of Birmingham, woodcuts by Bewick of Newcastle, and aquatint engraving at the peak

OAKLY PARK, SHROPSHIRE Above left: *The conservatory designed by C. R. Cockerell.*

TATTON PARK, CHESHIRE Above: *Lewis Wyatt's drawing room on the east side of the house retains its original rich furnishing by Gillow.*

WILLEY PARK, SHROPSHIRE Right: *Designed by Lewis Wyatt for the 1st Lord Forester, in 1812.*

of perfection. Both finely illustrated folio volumes and loose albums of prints for general delectation were displayed on large tables, which were the centrepiece of many libraries.

The dining room became the other distinctively English interior in this period, with its own features and particular furniture. The dining room had emerged in the eighteenth century in response to particular English social conditions. Robert Adam in the *Works in Architecture* (1773–79) remarked on this and differentiated English practice from the French, who did not have eating rooms in their great apartments. In England, however, climate, love of the bottle, and the political constitution made the men congregate more to drink and discuss parliamentary matters, therefore 'eating rooms are considered as the apartments of conversation, in which we … pass a great part of our time.' As a result they were treated as principal rooms of the house, with consonant architectural decoration.

The Regency saw the apotheosis of the English dining room, in both scale and splendour. The later hour of dining led to particular architectural developments. Whereas Adam and early Wyatt dining rooms had been rather summery rooms with pastel shades and elaborate stucco decorations, intended to be seen by daylight, the Regency dining room was usually decorated in a darker palette, crimson being a favourite hue, as it was intended to be seen at night, lit by candelabra and Colza oil lamps or even gas (all Regency introductions).

For the same reason, there was often a stronger, more monumental form of decoration, sometimes marmoreal in character as at Dodington, Goodwood, Belvoir and Chatsworth. The Regency dining room was also much larger than its Georgian predecessors, necessary to accommodate thirty or forty house guests plus extra invited neighbours for dinner. The Earl of Derby's new dining room, added to Knowsley in 1820 to the design of Foster of Liverpool, was 53 feet long and, according to Creevey, 'such a height that it destroys the effect of all the other apartments'. It was entered through doors 30 feet high. 'Pray are those great doors to be opened for every pat of butter that comes into the room?' queried General Grosvenor.

Like the library, the Regency dining room had its own distinctive furniture, nearly always solidly constructed of mahogany. This

BROUGHTON HALL, YORKSHIRE Above: *The conservatory.*

MELDON PARK, NORTHUMBERLAND Right: *The conservatory designed by John Dobson.*

included a large patent dining table capable of being extended and contracted, with endless spare leaves, and sets of specialist subsidiary tables, serving tables and wine tables, and monumental sideboards. The sideboard as an integrated piece of furniture with cupboards and drawers was an English Regency invention, developed out of the late-Georgian arrangement of a side-table flanked by free-standing pedestals for urns. The sideboard was frequently built in and formed part of the architecture of the room, as in the state dining rooms at Belvoir or Windsor Castle.

Another innovation in Regency houses was the provision of large numbers of comfortable, informal guest bedrooms: suites with dressing rooms for married couples, and long runs of smaller 'bachelor bedrooms' for single male guests – as in the north wing at Chatsworth, and the east wing at Arundel. The most lavish provision of guest rooms was at Windsor Castle, where George IV, ever in the forefront, provided suites of guest rooms with sitting rooms and bathrooms adjoining – twenty-eight rooms on the principal floor of the south wing alone.

Regency bedrooms were often charmingly decorated with chintz or calico, English industrial productions from the cotton mills of Lancashire; hung with Chinese wallpaper imported by the East India Company; or displaying watercolours by Copley Fielding, Cotman, Girtin, Prout, Hunt, Varley and their contemporaries, which were thought particularly apt for bedrooms. They were furnished with writing tables, wash-stands, chests of drawers, wardrobes (another Regency furnishing innovation), comfortable chairs and sofas, matching sets of washing china (another new fashion) and heated by blazing fires, for they were not intended just for sleeping but for general occupation. Many women, and guests, stayed in their rooms all morning until noon, scribbling away in journals or writing letters. Large numbers of Regency bedrooms still survive in country houses as they are so charming and comfortable that nobody has ever wanted to change them.

The incorporation of a conservatory into the house was also a new development in this period. There are earlier examples of orangeries being attached to houses, as at Dyrham Park in Gloucestershire, but the regular incorporation of a greenhouse or conservatory adjoining the living rooms was distinctively Regency and was strongly taken up by the Wyatts at Dodington, Ashridge, Willey, Chatsworth, and elsewhere. Nash, too, was keen on conservatories and included three in his remodelling of Buckingham Palace. The most spectacular example was the cast-iron Gothic conservatory, inspired by Henry VII's Chapel, added to Carlton House by the Prince Regent in 1807 and designed by Thomas Hopper, which helped to popularise the concept and also propelled its architect to fashionable notice.

The use of cast iron at Carlton House was not exceptional. Nash made structural use of cast iron at Brighton Pavilion and Buckingham Palace, as did Smirke at Lowther. The Wyatts, with their Midlands industrial connections, had always used 'new' materials, including Coade stone, Roman cement, metal alloy glazing bars, rolled copper roofing and other advanced products of English manufacturing. The

Regency country house was the mature product of the first Industrial Revolution and, whatever its style, was filled with new inventions, gadgets and manufactures: Colza oil lamps, all kinds of patent iron grates and stoves, Bramah water closets, central heating, occasional hot baths, steam-pumped water supplies and kitchen gadgetry, and towards the end of the period, gas lighting. Carlton House, Brighton Pavilion and Dodington were all part gas lit before the 1820s.

These innovations, as well as making houses more comfortable, also made possible particular architectural features, especially full-height atrium-like halls, and impressive imperial-plan staircases (leading only to bedrooms) which were such a feature of houses like Belsay, Meldon, Dodington and Willey Park. Without some degree of artificial heating, houses like Ashridge or Penrhyn, with their ludicrously tall entrance and staircase halls, would have been uninhabitable in winter.

The specialised planning and unprecedented comfort of the Regency house, its incorporation of new technology and industrial materials, are perhaps overshadowed by its lushly Picturesque setting and the extreme and adventurous eclecticism of its architecture. Gothic, Norman, Hindu, Greek, Roman, Italianate, Tudorbethan, Thatched 'Old English', French 'Louis Quatorze', Chinese, Egyptian – all can be found in the houses built in England between 1800 and 1830. Sometimes there were several styles in the same building at once, as at Belvoir, which, for that reason, Christopher Hussey dubbed 'the apotheosis of Regency taste'. This restless stylistic incontinence is a manifestation of the power of fashion (noted by Pückler-Muskau). Novelty and richness were what mattered, and the pace was set by the Prince Regent, who rearranged, remodelled and redecorated Carlton House every few months, creating new effects for the smart world to copy which then filtered down through the publications of Smith, Papworth and Loudon and their ilk.

Like mountain peaks part concealed by foothills, above and behind all this architectural froth certain predominant stylistic strands can be discerned: on the one hand a rich Graeco-Roman Classical style, and on the other a dry, somewhat paste-board though archaeologically

inspired Gothic based on indigenous Perpendicular sources – a proto-national style. Both these were invented by James Wyatt, whose work is in many ways a precursor of the Regency style. He pioneered the strong marble-inspired colours and the extensive use of *scagliola* which became such a dominant aspect of Regency taste, as originally demonstrated in the ground-floor rooms he remodelled for the Prince Regent at Carlton House, and in the hall and dining room at Dodington, where he worked continuously from 1795 until his death in 1813. This style was perpetuated in the work of his sons and nephews, Benjamin Dean and Philip, Jeffry and Lewis to the end of the period.

John Nash, Thomas Cundy and Thomas Hopper adopted the same styles but in a coarser, more slapdash and theatrical way, as did Wyatt pupils like William Atkinson or Foster of Liverpool and pupils of pupils like Webster of Kendal. Robert Smirke specialised in new castles for Tory grandees, of which Lowther is now a shell, but Eastnor in Herefordshire survives in fine order. William Wilkins could do Greek or

Tudor: on the one hand, the Parthenon-like Grange in Hampshire for the Baring Bankers (never photographed by *Country Life*), and on the other Tregothnan, a 'Tudor' essay for the Earl of Falmouth on a Cornish seaside site. C. R. Cockerell brought intellect, originality and a refined taste to the Greek Revival, as can be seen at Oakly Park, Shropshire – the remodelling of a standard Georgian brick box.

The greatest architect of the age, Sir John Soane, did very little country house work after 1800 apart from his own house at Pitzhanger, and Port Eliot, Wotton, Moggerhanger and Pell Wall. They all deployed his personal and idiosyncratic Roman Classical manner. The first four survive, but Pell Well Hall in Staffordshire is now a shell and has never been covered in *Country Life*. His major domestic jobs were largely executed in the 1780s and 1790s. Tyringham, for example, was designed in 1793. After 1800 he was mainly occupied with public commissions for the latter part of his career.

The architectural interest of the Regency country house, however, derives above all from its variety and richness, the way it relates to its landscaped setting, and the quality of the materials and craftsmanship. The interiors are also, for the first time in English architecture, as much the work of decorators as of architects, relying on strong colour,

CRONKHILL, SHROPSHIRE Above: *A small Italianate villa by John Nash, 1802.*
WOTTON HOUSE, BUCKINGHAMSHIRE Left: *The entrance hall by John Soane, 1820.*

carpets, upholstery and curtains, as in William Porden's Eaton Hall which was a triumph of the 'upholder's art'. This, of course, followed the example of the Regent himself, who spent thirty years obliterating Holland's refined Louis XVI interiors at Carlton House and transforming them into a decorator's paradise of silk, velvet, tassels and Garter blue carpets.

At Windsor Castle, the rooms were under the control of Morel & Seddon, furniture makers and decorators. Wyatville, the architect, had little to do with much of the interior finishing and, reading between the lines, actually disapproved of the French fittings and overgilding of the rooms desired by George IV. 'It is His Majesty's taste', he responded laconically to the parliamentary commissioners when questioned about the expensive decoration at the castle. This dominance of the decorator in the Regency interior is another of the ways in which the Regency country house seems to parallel our own times.

The Regency country house was well built. The upper echelons of the building world were dominated by certain firms who are encountered again and again in different places. The Wyatts in particular were responsible for training up an army of skilled craftsmen and suppliers who came to dominate, almost mass-produce, the Regency house – Bernasconi for plasterwork, Alcott & Browne for *scagliola*, Edward Wyatt himself for carving, Gillow for furniture, and Birmingham for all kinds of metalwork.

Regency craftsmanship has the slight deadness of too great a perfection: moulded rather than hand-modelled plaster, machine-cut stone and marble with joints calculated to several decimal places. This is all admirable but not lovable; it can have an excessive hardness of finish and a repetitiveness of detail which endows a house, like Ashridge or the exteriors of Windsor and Eastnor, with an institutional feel when viewed with a post-Arts and Crafts movement sensibility. To contemporaries, however, that hard perfection was a goal to strive for and prize. The rich taste and fashionable whims of the Prince Regent and the architectural industry of the Wyatt clan were two key factors in the development of the Regency style. Another was the propaganda of a single-minded amateur: Thomas Hope, a rich Dutch banker of Scottish descent, who set about improving English taste in interior decoration and promoting astonishingly archaeological furniture for ordinary domestic use.

Combining Grecian forms, French Empire splendour and Egyptian motifs – an amalgam of Stuart and Revett's *The Antiquities of Athens*, Percier & Fontaine, and Denon's *Egypte* – Hope created a highly successful furniture style, using rich, varied exotic woods and ormolu mounts. Soon, every chair in England had Grecian sabre legs and every table lotus-leaf moulding, while draped and tasselled curtains held up by eagles and tent beds became ubiquitous. He achieved this partly through his own well-advertised houses at Duchess Street in London and The Deepdene in Surrey, but more particularly through his publication *Household Furniture and Interior Decoration*, which came out in 1807. Sidney Smith jocularly christened Hope 'the man of chairs and tables, the gentleman of sofas', but *Household Furniture* created a style, and Hope was as influential in popularising a fashion as Horace Walpole – another shrewd self-publicist – had been with Gothick at Strawberry Hill.

Hope was doubly successful: not only did he have influence in his own lifetime, but he had a large role in the twentieth-century Regency Revival. The sale of his collection at The Deepdene, in September 1917, was a key element in the rediscovery of 'Regency', in which *Country Life* itself was to play a strong part in the inter-war years through the writings of Christopher Hussey, the architectural editor, who detected a 'kinship between Regency and modern taste', and Margaret Jourdain, who pioneered the study of Regency furniture.

Apart from the rich eclecticism of grand Regency houses and smart decorative style, which have been remarked on, there was another side to the architecture of the period. This was a simple, often astylar, manner with large windows opening down to the ground. Such houses were simply finished in white painted stucco or smooth ashlar, with shallow roofs and flat parapets, like Bignor Park in Sussex and Meldon in Northumberland, or much of the work of Sir John Soane.

Such undemonstrative houses, where Classicism was mainly displayed in the proportions, seemed not unlike early Modern Movement buildings by Gropius or Mies van der Rohe. To some architectural commentators, they provided inspiration for a way forward, a springing-off point for a new style, going back to a simple, harmonious, clear-cut architecture before the encrusted barnacles of the Victorian battle of styles and the full-blown Gothic Revival. This was not just a Neo-Georgian viewpoint: many progressive British Modern architects in the twentieth century were inspired by Regency design. The late Sir James Stirling, for instance, architect of the Cambridge History Faculty and Stuttgart Museum, collected Thomas Hope and other Regency furniture.

The Regency Revival began before the First World War, when it was called 'English Empire' and was one of the gamut of styles used to decorate Mayfair houses and grand hotels. David Watkin has described this as 'Percier & Fontaine seen … through a rich haze of brandy fumes and cigar smoke'. There was a similar revival in France. Readers of Proust will remember that the Hôtel Guermantes is suddenly rearranged to include chairs decorated with swans' heads like bath taps, previously despised. The English revival owed something to this smart Parisian background.

Edward Knoblock, a key figure and the rediscoverer of Thomas Hope, lived in Paris before the First World War. He was a Henry James type of rich cosmopolitan American, and indeed was a personal friend of the writer. Born in 1874, he arrived in London in 1897, but went to Paris for a couple of years around 1912 where he decorated a pioneering apartment in the Empire style in the Palais Royal. Shortly before 1914, he returned to London where he took rooms in Albany and these were done up for him by the architect Maxwell Ayrton, with marbled walls and Regency furniture. This was the first example of informed and scholarly Regency Revival in England.

SEZINCOTE, GLOUCESTERSHIRE Right: *Shrine to Sourya, the sun god. The statue is of Coade stone, a manufactured material used widely in Regency buildings.*

Though a pioneer with strongly pronounced interests in Regency furniture and decoration, Knoblock was not an isolated figure, and other connoisseurs of furniture and young architects were rediscovering the English late-Georgian tradition at the same time. Albert Richardson published his *Monumental Classic Architecture in England* in 1914. This seminal work was responsible for the revival of the English Classical manner in the twentieth century. The Irish Georgian Society had also been founded in Dublin in 1910 to promote interest in Irish eighteenth- and early-nineteenth-century architecture. When Richardson and Eberlein published *The Smaller English House of the Later Renaissance 1660–1830* in 1925, it is notable that they included a great deal of Regency architecture, and Richardson himself collected Regency furniture and decorated his houses accordingly from early in his career. In 1909, he had bought a Regency house for himself, Cavendish House in St Albans, and in 1919 he moved to the late-Georgian Avenue House in Ampthill, Bedfordshire, with a splendid Regency drawing room, where he lived for the rest of his life.

By the mid-1920s, Regency was fashionable and Queen Mary, with the advice of Clifford Smith of the Victoria & Albert Museum, was busy sorting out George IV's furniture at Windsor and Buckingham Palace into the original sets, rehanging vast glass chandeliers, and making Regency purchases and additions of her own, such as the Vulliamy chimneypieces in the Bow Room, and Thomas Hope-inspired wall lights in the Grand Hall at Buckingham Palace.

At the Christie's sale of the Hope Heirlooms at The Deepdene in 1917, Knoblock was able to take advantage of the uninformed cataloguing and acquired many of the key pieces of Thomas Hope furniture. He then bought Beach House, Worthing, on the Sussex coast, in 1918 – a plain nineteenth-century villa – which was done up for him by Maxwell Ayrton as the most complete Regency statement of its time, with marbling, French landscape wallpapers, draped curtains, and Hope furniture. This was the first Regency house to be covered by *Country Life*, in January 1921.

The author was the young Christopher Hussey who had joined the architectural team at *Country Life* the year before, after Eton and Oxford. His family background gave him a strong interest in the Regency period. His great-grandmother's house was Oakly Park in Shropshire by C. R. Cockerell, and his grandfather's house, which he was to inherit, Scotney Castle, Kent, was a masterpiece of early-nineteenth-century Picturesque. Though early Victorian in date (begun to the design of Anthony Salvin in 1837), Scotney was in the Regency landscape tradition and inspired Hussey's pioneering researches into the Picturesque, first expressed in an article on Dunglass near Haddington in Scotland in 1925.

Over the years, *Country Life,* under Hussey's direction, covered many of the major Regency country houses. In 1922, it published a piece lamenting the destruction of Nash's own house in Lower Regent Street. In 1924, articles appeared on James Wyatt's Dodington in Gloucestershire; in 1926, on Willey Park; in 1928, on Soane's Tyringham, and the Regency furniture at Southill; in 1930, on George IV's Windsor Castle; in 1931, on 'Four Regency Houses' in London; in

---

Above: *Designs by Gillow for window and bed curtains demonstrate the elaboration of Regency upholstery.*

CRANBURY PARK, HAMPSHIRE Left: *The Tent Room by J. B. Papworth. Military tent rooms were a characteristic Regency fashion inspired by the Napoleonic Wars.*

1932, on Goodwood; in 1934, on Albert Richardson's Avenue House, Ampthill; in 1935, on Mount Stewart, Co. Down; in 1936, on Panshanger, an Atkinson house, still then with its staggering picture gallery intact, and in the 1940s, on Grimston in Yorkshire, Belsay, Northumberland and Highcliffe Castle in Hampshire. In 1948, sympathetic articles dwell on the new Duke of Wellington's rearrangement of Regency Stratfield Saye. In the 1950s, Hussey systematically covered all the major remaining Regency houses, with an eye to a volume in his *Country Life* trilogy, *Late Georgian 1800–1840*, published in 1958. He prolonged his period into the early Victorian years in order to include Salvin's early work, notably Hussey's own beloved Scotney.

By the 1930s, let alone the 1950s, Regency, which had been thought ugly by some, was ultra-fashionable – Osbert Lancaster mocked the Revival as 'Vogue Regency' in *Home Sweet Homes* in 1939, and the plates from Thomas Hope's *Household Furniture* were reprinted by John Tiranti Ltd. In 1937, the final seal was put on the Revival by Clifford Musgrave's restoration and refurnishing of Brighton Pavilion and the annual Regency Exhibitions held there from 1948 onwards, borrowing from the Royal Collection and other sources.

The 'Four Regency Houses' published in *Country Life* in 1931, included 11 Montagu Terrace, Knoblock's new house where he had redeployed the Hope furniture, and also 11 Titchfield Street, the house of Lord Gerald Wellesley, later 7th Duke of Wellington, which had been done up by him in Regency taste in the 1920s. Gerry Wellesley was a school contemporary and close friend of Christopher Hussey's. They shared a house in the country until Hussey married. Wellesley had a particularly strong affinity with the Regency period because of his great ancestor, and he shared these enthusiasms with Hussey.

As an architect, like several of his contemporaries – Darcy Braddell and Hal Goodhart-Rendel – Wellesley saw Regency as the inspiration for a twentieth-century English style, and this affected Hussey's approach and the way in which *Country Life* assessed and described Regency buildings. As the last pre-Victorian phase of architecture, Christopher Hussey saw it as having parallels with the Modern Movement, and providing a basis for developing a clean, modern

Classical architecture for the future. He wrote in 1931: 'It is this kinship between Regency and modern taste (the product of similar social conditions) that is the real cause of the imputation of audacity to modern Regency bucks … It must always be remembered that Regency was the last recognisable style that furniture designers employed before the great debacle of Victorianism. It is thus one of the natural points of departure into the future and quite the best.' As the Classical architect Raymond Erith put it in a letter to Hussey in 1934: 'I feel that pure modern is happier in London, if flavoured with Regency and urns.'

This attitude needs to be understood when looking at the photographs in the following pages. They were taken partly to illustrate an architectural campaign and have to be seen through Regency Revival eyes. Several of the houses featured in *Country Life* in the 1920s and 1930s had been recently redecorated and refurnished by twentieth-century Regency aficionados and collectors like Thomas Upcher at Sheringham, Lord Ismay at Wormington or Lord Mersey at Bignor, while in others, squashy sofas and non-Regency clutter have been ruthlessly removed from the rooms to create a sabre-legged vision of Regency perfection. The 1899 *Country Life* photographs of The Deepdene show what Regency interiors were really like before Knoblock, Hussey, Richardson, Wellesley *et al* got to work on them and created our modern image of the Regency house.

PANSHANGER, HERTFORDSHIRE Top left: *The Regency picture gallery.*

THE BEACH HOUSE, SUSSEX Above: *Bookcase designed by Thomas Hope and acquired by Edward Knoblock from The Deepdene sale, 1917.*

Right: *Egyptian chair designed by Thomas Hope, in the Knoblock collection, photographed by* Country Life *in 1921.*

1 THE PALACES

UNDER George IV, palace building was a major strand of English architectural activity for the first time since the Stuarts. Carlton House, George IV's palace when he was Prince of Wales and Prince Regent, was demolished in 1826–27 (two workmen being killed on the job), and his Royal Lodge has also gone, but three major houses remain: Windsor Castle, Buckingham Palace and Brighton Pavilion. These represent Regency taste in architecture and decoration at its grandest and most overblown. As King, George IV was determined to provide himself with a setting of a splendour and grandeur 'commensurate with his dignity as the constitutional head of the most powerful country in the world'. With the assistance of pliable architects – Nash and Wyatville – and vastly generous government funding (swelled by the repayment of the Austrian War Loan and the profits of the Crown Estates' successful Metropolitan Improvements in London), he succeeded where his immediate Hanoverian predecessors and their architects had so signally failed.

Brighton was, perhaps, more of a fantastic *plaisance* than a state palace and was disposed of by Queen Victoria early in her reign, but Buckingham Palace and Windsor Castle have remained the principal state residences of the British monarchy ever since, and still retain the fabulous collections which the King brought together to furnish and decorate them. In their rooms, it is still possible to savour the impact of the King's taste and the impression it made on his contemporaries.

In addition to George IV's extant royal palaces, three other exceptional houses were on such a princely scale of magnificence that they too count as palaces, even judged by the noblest standards – Chatsworth, Ashridge and Belvoir. The 6th Duke of Devonshire, who remodelled Chatsworth, was Lord Chamberlain. Some of his contemporaries thought he would be an ideal consort for Princess Charlotte, heir to the throne. Tsar Nicholas I of Russia was a great personal friend and inspired many of the Duke's architectural projects.

The 5th Duke of Rutland was descended from the Plantaganets, as was his wife – a Howard of Castle Howard – but more to the point, she was the close friend of the Duke of York (George IV's brother) and his amanuensis in architectural matters, so that her work at Belvoir was closely related to the projects of George IV's Court.

The 7th Earl of Bridgewater at Ashridge had megalomaniac tendencies, which he was able to indulge thanks to the great inheritance from the Canal Duke. Ashridge had been a royal property after the Dissolution of the Monasteries, until required in 1604 by Sir Thomas Egerton, from whom the Earl of Bridgewater was descended. Elizabeth I had lived there during the reign of Queen Mary. The royal and monastic associations played a part in the inspiration for the vast new Gothic palace on the site.

CHATSWORTH, DERBYSHIRE Above: *The entrance screen. This severe tripartite Roman Doric gateway was designed by Wyatville for the access court at Chatsworth. The principal triumphal arch in the middle is the main entrance, the smaller arches to left and right are to the kitchen offices and private west door respectively.*

BELVOIR CASTLE, LEICESTERSHIRE Left: *View over the Vale of Belvoir from the top of the Regent Tower with James Wyatt's octagonal chapel turrets in the foreground.*

BRIGHTON PAVILION Preceding pages: *The exterior at night, photographed by Alex Starkey in 1964 for the Country Life Annual. The stucco and Bath stonework conceal extensive structural use of cast iron.*

❧ WINDSOR CASTLE ❧

Windsor Castle, as reconstructed by Jeffry Wyatville from 1824 onwards, was the grandest architectural project of the period and the culmination of a life time of creating impressive residences on the part of King George IV. He moved in at the end of 1828, held his first big house party at New Year 1829, and died in his new bedroom there in 1830.

When George IV ascended the throne at the age of fifty-seven in 1820, he found Windsor part modernised and re-Gothicked, especially the state apartments, by his father under James Wyatt's direction. The south and east sides of the quadrangle, however, although containing one or two fine new rooms made for his mother, Queen Charlotte, were uncomfortable, inconvenient and ramshackle. He first stayed at the castle in 1823 and started to think about improvements with the advice of his friends, the Duke of Devonshire and Sir Charles Long (Lord Farnborough), an *éminence grise* of the artistic world in George IV's reign. The Duke recommended Jeffry Wyatt on the strength of his work at Chatsworth, and Lord Farnborough drew up a programme of improvements, including adding 30 feet to the Round

Tower to improve the skyline; contriving a corridor or gallery around the east and south sides of the quadrangle to link the private rooms to the state apartments; making a new entrance from the Long Walk; and completing the Gothicisation.

Various political intrigues followed, but the government soon pledged a generous sum of money for the work (to be vastly exceeded in the event), and after a limited 'competition', Wyatt (soon to be Wyatville, the name he assumed in 1824) got the job. The foundation

---

Above: *The Grand Corridor. Designed by Wyatville, this spacious gallery nearly 500 feet long linked the new visitors' apartments in the south range with the sitting rooms in the east and the state apartments in the north. Visitors were struck by its novel furnishing. Greville thought it more like a drawing room than a corridor. The busts and pictures were arranged under the King's direct supervision, with the advice of Sir David Wilkie and Sir Francis Chantrey.*

Right: *The Crimson Drawing Room. The magnificent gilded ceiling was designed by Wyatville and moulded by Francis Bernasconi, the leading stuccoist of the Regency age. The original crimson damask velvet (woven by W. & E. King) in gilt wall panels, mirrors and the gilded seat furniture were supplied by Morel & Seddon, the King's decorators, while the carved and gilt doors by Edward Wyatt, black marble chimneypiece by Vulliamy and the various candelabra all came from Carlton House.*

stone of the new George IV Gateway at the top of Charles II's extended Long Walk was laid by the King with a silver trowel in 1824. Wyatville carried out all of Long's programme, creating the marvellous silhouette of the castle so admired today, and converting a medieval warren into a well-planned house.

The King took a particularly strong interest in the decoration and furnishing of the new royal apartments in the south and east wings. These were planned by Wyatville, who also designed in detail the ceilings and the Gothic halls and galleries. The wall treatment of the main rooms was finished under the King's personal direction and strongly reflected his life-long Francophile tastes – the style chosen was an ultra-rich combination of Empire and Louis XIV, executed by the decorators Morel & Seddon.

These impressive apartments contained chimneypieces, carved doors, furnishings, chandeliers and even some of the silk from Carlton House (demolished in 1825). Much more was made anew at prodigious expense by Morel & Seddon's team, which included the silk mercers W. & E. King and several French craftsmen, notably the famous Parisian *ébéniste* F. H. G. Jacob-Desmalter. These rooms therefore are a significant demonstration of the rise of the interior decorator and the triumph of upholstery in the early-nineteenth-century interior.

George IV's work at Windsor was greatly admired at the time, and – on the whole – has been ever since. Pückler-Muskau wrote: 'It is a vast work and the only one of its kind in England which is executed not only at a great cost and with technical skill but with uncommon taste, nay genius.

'The magnificence of the interior corresponds with the exterior …, and the eye is dazzled with velvet, silk and gilding. I must confess that the internal decorations, spite of all their gorgeousness, appeared to me to leave much to wish for. They are enormously overloaded in parts, and are not always either in keeping with the character of the building.' Most visitors, however, were impressed by the magnificence of the rooms. Princess Lieven (not always easy to please) thought the rooms 'magnificent in the extreme' and that 'luxury can hardly be carried further, and comfort is equally well looked to; in short, nothing is left to be desired.'

They have survived with little serious alteration for nearly two hundred years; while fire damage in the State Dining Room and Crimson Drawing Room in 1992 has since been immaculately restored. The photographs here were taken in 1952 to mark the accession of Queen Elizabeth II and include some of the first colour photographs to be published by *Country Life*.

The Green Drawing Room (Library). The most distinguished of the George IV rooms, this was originally a typical Regency library-living room, but the books were removed later to the new Royal Library in the north-west corner of the castle. The rosewood and ormolu cases, extended to match, came from Carlton House, as did the chimneypiece and the gilt doors carved by Edward Wyatt, some of the furniture and the bronzes. The original green satin on the walls from W. & E. King, silk mercers, the mirrors and the seat furniture were supplied by Morel & Seddon.

Above: *The boudoir. The same combination of richly modelled plasterwork
and French elegance of decoration was extended by Wyatville and Morel & Seddon
into the smaller private apartments.*

Left: *The White Drawing Room (Small Drawing Room). The ceiling was designed by
Wyatville and executed by Bernasconi. The ebony-and-ormolu-framed mirror doors were
supplied by Morel & Seddon in 1828 and are thought to be by Jacob-Desmalter.
The black marble and ormolu chimneypiece and candelabra came from Carlton House.*

≳ BRIGHTON PAVILION ≲

The Prince of Wales first visited Brighton in September 1783 with his uncle the Duke of Cumberland, whom George III considered a bad influence. The Prince loved the free and raffish environment, the racing and cricket; and Brighton became a regular part of his annual calendar. In 1785 (the year he secretly married Mrs Fitzherbert), he commissioned Henry Holland to design a 'marine pavilion' in French Neo-Classical taste on the site of a small farmhouse overlooking the Steine, a strip of grassland at right angles to the sea. The Prince's Westphalian cook Louis Weltje, another of his chef-connoisseurs, like François Benois the confectioner at Carlton House, directed the work and bought French furniture for the interior.

After 1800, the Prince decided to transform the Marine Pavilion into a 'Chinese' building. According to the local historian E. W. Brayley (writing thirty years later), this was in response to the gift of some 'very beautiful' Chinese wallpaper. Holland's pupil, P. F. Robinson, produced some unexecuted pagoda-inspired proposals. A further change of stylistic direction occurred in 1804, when William

Porden designed the huge stable block and domed riding school (with a roof similar to the Halle au Blé in Paris) sporting Saracenic elevations. These completely overshadowed Holland's modest Pavilion, and introduced a hint of Asia into the Brighton landscape; a year later the Prince decided to remodel it to match Porden's stables. Porden had been introduced to the Prince by a racing crony, Lord Grosvenor, for whom Porden was reconstructing Eaton Hall in Cheshire at the same time (*see pages 86–9*).

As architect for reconstructing the Pavilion, the Prince turned to Humphry Repton, who suggested the fashionable style of Hindustan, but by 1815 Repton had been superseded by his erstwhile partner

Above: *The gallery. An innovation of the Prince Regent's was to furnish access galleries as sitting rooms, a concept which received its highest form in the Grand Corridor at Windsor. The pink and blue chinoiserie wall decorations were executed by Frederick Crace. The staircases at either end were made of cast iron to simulate bamboo.*

Right: *Saloon door. The form of the circular saloon in the centre of the Pavilion survived from Holland's original house, but was overlaid by Nash's fusion of Indian and chinoiserie.*

John Nash, who drew up a scheme for an Oriental fantasy palace. Holland's Pavilion was kept at the centre, but flanked by additions incorporating vast banqueting and music rooms and new kitchens. The old building was stuccoed and disguised by fretted verandahs of Bath stone, and the skyline enlivened with bulbous onion domes and slender minarets. The details for this external Indian transformation were derived from William Daniell's *Oriental Scenery*, published in 1795. (Nash borrowed the Prince's own copy from the Carlton House library to use as a crib.)

Building work continued into the 1820s. The structure of the domes was of cast iron, so that the remodelled Pavilion was characteristically Regency, both in its use of advanced industrial materials and its effervescent stylistic adventurousness. The Prince Regent's work at Brighton gave a new lease of life to the Georgian vogue for chinoiserie and is also a striking demonstration of the romantic stylistic plurality, which is a major aspect of Regency architecture in England. The Pavilion itself, though, was such a personal and scenic extravaganza that it had few direct imitations. Sezincote, the other Hindu-style house (which Repton had recommended as a model for Brighton), was a precursor rather than a copy and was built for a director of the East India Company. It, too, was derived architecturally from Daniell's depictions of Indian buildings.

The inside of Brighton was kitted out in an exuberant mix of chinoiserie and Indian, which was brilliantly successful and, like all the Prince Regent's works, displayed superb craftsmanship. The interior, too, made structural use of cast iron, such as the main staircase with its pierced iron treads and balustrades moulded to simulate bamboo, or the iron columns in the kitchen with leaf capitals to represent slender palm trees.

Many of the Chinese details were culled from William Alexander's *Views of China*, published in 1805, such as the red and gold 'lacquered' walls and silvered dragons of the new music room. The lotus-flower chandeliers in this room were produced by Perry & Co. and were more Indian in derivation; their scale, elaboration and brilliance of light caused amazement. The furniture, by Bailey and Saunders, fused the Grecian forms – found in the Prince's Carlton House seat furniture – with chinoiserie detail. The domed or tented ceilings in this and the banqueting room were designed by Nash and were unprecedented in English architecture. The gilding was carried out in four shades of gold by Frederick Crace & Son, who were responsible for most of the decoration at the Pavilion.

The banqueting room was an even more glittering ensemble than the music room. The stupendous chandelier, weighing one ton, comprised six lotus-flower lamps suspended from a large winged dragon and painted copper plantain tree. Around the room were standing Sèvres-blue porcelain *torchères* manufactured by Spode; they represented the pinnacle of English technology and craftsmanship.

The saloon as furnished by Clifford Musgrave, with borrowed items for the annual Regency Exhibition, which began in 1948.

Above: *The banqueting room. This vast chandelier, with six lotus lamps seemingly suspended from a dragon's claws, weighs one ton and was supplied by Perry & Co., the leading purveyors of chandeliers of the Regency period. They were also responsible for the crystal 'fountain pattern' chandeliers at Carlton House, now at Windsor Castle and Buckingham Palace.*

Right: *The banqueting room. A colour photograph taken in 1962 for* Country Life's *Collector's Number showing the room set out for the Regency Exhibition, an annual summer event inaugurated in 1948.*

The white marble chimneypiece with ormolu mounts was supplied by Richard Westmacott (Junior) and the walls painted with chinoiserie scenes in panels by Robert Jones.

Brighton Pavilion was at the forefront of contemporary technology. In 1821, gas lighting was introduced, making it one of the first domestic interiors in the world to be lit by gas. The scheme was devised by the pioneer gas entrepreneur Frederick Winsor, who illuminated the exterior of Carlton House with gas as early as 1808 and founded the Gas-light & Coke Company. The Prince's support for Winsor was responsible for the widespread nineteenth-century adoption of gas lighting in England from the late Regency period onwards. The kitchen technology at Brighton was equally progressive and made use of steam both for heating and for driving spits and other devices. In 1816, the Prince had acquired the great French cook Antoine Carême (formerly in the employ of Talleyrand), who produced hundred-dish dinners for the Prince's guests in the Brighton kitchen. Over-lit, over-heated and over-fed, a Brighton house party represented the acme of modern luxury.

Contemporary comments combined shock and awe with ironic amusement. Pückler-Muskau, who visited in 1827, noted: 'The King was formerly very fond of Brighton and built a strange Oriental Palace which seen from the adjoining heights, with its cupolas and minarets looks exactly like the pieces on a chess board. The interior is splendidly though fantastically furnished.' Hazlitt left a more entertaining description: 'The pavilion at Brighton is like a collection of stone pumpkins and pepper boxes. It seems as if the genius of architecture has at once the dropsy and the megrims.' Grumpy William Cobbett was funniest of all: 'Take a considerable number of bulbs of the Crown Imperial, the narcissus, the hyacinth, the tulip, the crocus and others; let the leaves of each have sprouted to about one inch ... then stand off and look at your architecture. There! That's a "Kremlin"! Only you must cut some church-looking windows in the sides of the box. As to what you ought to put into the box that is a subject far above my cut.'

Queen Victoria disliked the Pavilion with its lack of privacy and sold it to Brighton Corporation in 1850. Many of the chimneypieces and fittings were removed to Buckingham Palace, where they were re-assembled to create an unlikely group of Victorian chinoiserie rooms. Against expectation, however, Brighton Corporation did not demolish the Pavilion. In the twentieth century, its gradual restoration and refurnishing, especially under the directorship of Clifford Musgrave, played a large part in the modern revival of interest in Regency architecture and decorative arts.

Top right: *The King's Bedroom. The King's private set of rooms were on the ground floor, to the left of the entrance hall, whereas the guest bedrooms were upstairs. The King's rooms were comparatively simple and originally decorated by Crace with green and silver chinoiserie wall paintings.*

Below right: *The music room door, with decoration by Frederick Crace & Son.*

Left: *The music room. This was one of two vast new reception rooms added after 1815 to Nash's design. The painted wall decorations were adapted from William Alexander's* Views of China *(1805). The lotus flower chandeliers were among the earliest in England to be lit by gas.*

≽ BUCKINGHAM PALACE ≼

Concealed behind the pomp of Aston Webb's early twentieth-century façade, the gilded railings and the red coated sentries – every child's idea of the perfect palace – lies George IV's Neo-Classical reconstruction of his mother's house. Caught out of context, this could be a building in Potsdam, St Petersburg or Napoleonic Paris. Though sadly unfinished at the time of George IV's death (the victim of changes of mind and Nash's slapdash, if theatrical, design processes), it is nevertheless highly original in many ways and contains some of the contents – rich French furniture, vast glass chandeliers and superlative Dutch pictures – from Carlton House, the regal trailblazer of the Regency style. Together with the rooms at Windsor, the

CARLTON HOUSE Above: *An unexecuted scheme by John Nash for conversion into a state palace with large flanking blocks, a dome, pilasters and statues on the roof. Only the portico is a recognisable part of Henry Holland's original design. In the event, Carlton House was demolished in 1826, after George IV had transferred his attentions to Buckingham Palace.*

BUCKINGHAM PALACE Left above: *The entrance front designed by Nash (now concealed in the quadrangle). The two-tier porte-cochère and portico combine convenience with new technology and French architectural influence. The ground-floor Doric columns are of cast iron. The upper Corinthian Order is inspired by that of the Louvre. The trophies and statues on the roof were of artificial stone supplied by William Croggan but were removed in the mid-twentieth century. The ugly glass canopies are Edwardian additions.*

Left below: *The centre of the garden front. The domed bow was inspired by Rousseau's Hôtel de Salm in Paris, which had also been one of the architectural sources for Henry Holland's Carlton House. The plate glass in the principal windows was among the earliest uses of this new technology in England.*

Nash parts of Buckingham Palace still give an impression of why contemporaries were star-struck by the Prince Regent's interiors and architectural projects.

Throughout his adult life, the Prince had paid homage to French *ancien régime* taste and in the process did much to create the English Regency style in architecture and decoration. Though obviously inspired by Louis XVI sources in Paris – such as the Hôtel de Salm or the later Tuileries of Percier & Fontaine – together with backward glances at Versailles, this Francophile architecture in the Prince's hands and those of his succession of designers underwent a metamorphosis and emerged distinctively overblown. It was thanks partly to the capabilities of British industrial technology, whether cast-iron columns or Croggan's artificial stone, newly invented plate glass or Birmingham metal alloys. All this can be savoured on a surreal scale at Buckingham Palace. Behind the inflated opulence can still be seen the ghost of its chaster predecessor at Carlton House, and the two buildings, although one has been demolished and the other much remodelled, were key expressions of Regency style.

George III gave Carlton House, former residence of Frederick Prince of Wales, to his eldest son George when he came of age. It stood on what is now Waterloo Place and Duke of York Steps. The Prince began reconstructing it in 1783 with Henry Holland as his architect and various Frenchmen as decorators, including François Benois, Guillaume Gaubert, François Hervé and from 1787,

Dominique Daguerre, an émigré Parisian furniture dealer. After 1802, Holland was dropped and a succession of other architects were employed, including James Wyatt, John Nash and Thomas Hopper.

The rooms were redecorated with startling frequency, including the regular insertion of new chimneypieces. Between 1784 and 1819, for instance, the Bow Room (Rose Satin Drawing Room) had four consecutive chimneypieces. When it was first opened, Horace Walpole described Carlton House as the most perfect in Europe, and praised Henry Holland's achievement as a chaste palace: 'there is an august simplicity that astonished me ... it is the taste and propriety that strike.' Something of that quality can still be found at Southill,

Above: *The Grand Hall. The low proportions survive from old Buckingham House. Nash gave more height to the central area by excavating the floor. The Carrara marble pavement and columns and the original scagliola wall treatment (painted white in 1902) were all supplied by Joseph Browne.*

Right: *The picture gallery. A set of four Carrara marble chimneypieces designed by Nash were supplied by Joseph Browne. Each has a roundel portrait of a famous artist: this one shows Dürer. The Dutch paintings were collected by George IV.*

Opposite: *The entrée staircase. The top-lit space has one of Nash's domed and tented ceilings characteristic of the state rooms at Buckingham Palace. The rectangular plaster frieze panels, representing the four seasons, were designed by the painter Thomas Stothard and executed by his son Alfred. The lunettes were by Francis Bernasconi. The gilded bronze balustrade was made by Samuel Parker. The scrolling design is a masterpiece of English craftsmanship in metal.*

remodelled subsequently by Holland for Samuel Whitbread (*see pages 132–7*), but Carlton House itself was soon transmogrified into a more opulent and variegated ensemble.

In 1805, the Prince employed Walsh Porter, a picture dealer and one of the fashionable odd-balls with whom he liked to surround himself, to redecorate the interior. Joseph Farrington, the gossip of the Royal Academy, noted in his diary that the Prince and Walsh Porter had 'destroyed all that Holland has done', substituting a most 'motley taste', with brighter colours and exaggerated hangings and draperies. These sensational transformations had a great impact, and the fashionable architectural world rapidly followed suit.

The non-stop remodelling and redecoration of Carlton House only came to an end when the Prince finally lost interest after the celebration of the Allied victories in 1814–15. He toyed with the idea of remodelling Carlton House to Nash's design, adding a dome and framing it in a pair of large side wings, but the site facing Pall Mall was too constricted. After the death of his mother in 1818, he transferred his ambitions to the Queen's House at the other end of the Mall, and started badgering Lord Liverpool, the Prime Minister, for money to rebuild it. Nash produced his first designs in 1821. These envisaged a range of new rooms on the garden side, and encasing the whole in Bath stone, flanking it with new projecting wings, and fronting it with a double-height portico-porte-cochère on the entrance side.

As always with George IV, once work had started, his ambitions grew and what he at first claimed was merely a private residence for his old age, was soon transformed into a state palace. In 1825, the scale and grandeur were increased and the decision taken to demolish Carlton House. An important aspect of the revised scheme was that the remodelled palace would be a showcase for contemporary English sculpture, inside and out, with ornamental friezes, statues, trophies, chimneypieces and the March Arch – the main entrance in front – like Napoleon's Tuileries Arch in Paris.

The Arch was conceived as a monument to victory in the French Wars with friezes showing Trafalgar and Waterloo, all designed by John Flaxman and executed by Richard Westmacott (Junior) and Edward Hodges Baily. It was incomplete at the time of George IV's death and was moved in 1850 to its present ignominious site at the north end of Park Lane. Baily was also responsible for the pediment relief of *Britannia Acclaimed by Neptune*. Other reliefs on the entrance front were carved by J. E. Carew. Much of the architectural ornament

– including statues and trophies on the roof-line (taken down after the Second World War) – the friezes, capitals of columns and console brackets were modelled in artificial stone by William Croggan in 1827–28. He was the successor to Mrs Eleanor Coade, the Georgian female entrepreneur, who founded the artificial stone manufactory in Lambeth in 1769.

The emphasis on sculptural decoration was also a feature of the interior. The state rooms commissioned by George IV to Nash's design comprised a set of three new drawing rooms on the garden front, a central picture gallery, and a throne room on the site of Queen Charlotte's saloon, behind the portico, approached by a new grand staircase. The richness of their fixtures and fittings distinguishes them from any comparable set of rooms in England, and the originality of their architecture marks them out from contemporary palace rooms on the Continent. In their design they stretched the eighteenth-century Classical tradition to its limits to create an aura of extreme opulence.

The plaster ceilings, executed by Francis Bernasconi, were hailed by contemporaries as being out of the ordinary, with domes and convex or concave coving. The forms seem to have developed out of Nash's Mogul tent ceilings at Brighton Pavilion, and the eclectic Classical ornament derived from Ancient Greece and Rome, Napoleonic Paris and the Italian Renaissance. Friezes and tympana were filled with sculptured plaster reliefs, mainly modelled by the silver chaser William Pitts, although those in the throne room were designed by Thomas Stothard and modelled by E. H. Baily. The chimneypieces were by a cross-section of English sculptural talent, including M. C. Wyatt, R. W. Sievier and Richard Westmacott. The marblework and *scagliola*, which played a large part in the interior design, were executed under the supervision of Joseph Browne. Other unusual and expensive features were the mirror-plated doors and engraved glass skylights.

Many of these fixtures and fittings had not been installed at the time of George IV's death in 1830. Without the King's protection, Nash was censured for financial incompetence by Parliament and sacked. In 1832, Edward Blore was brought in to finish off the work as cheaply as possible, altering and watering down many of the details. Nash's vision has been further spoilt by inappropriate alterations at various dates in the twentieth century, but aspects of Buckingham Palace remain among the most impressive Regency architectural achievements.

A chinoiserie chimneypiece designed by Henry Holland for the Chinese Drawing Room at Carlton House. The private royal apartments at Buckingham Palace were fitted with chimneypieces originally made for Carlton House and salvaged when it was demolished in 1826. The inclusion of furnishings and fittings from Carlton House at Buckingham Palace, as at Windsor, emphasise its character as the successor to George IV's original residence.

⇒ CHATSWORTH, DERBYSHIRE ⇐

Chatsworth is two houses in one. As well as the 1st Duke of Devonshire's late-seventeenth-century Baroque quadrangle by Talman, Thornhill and Archer – with a west front inspired by Marly, a south front after Bernini, and a magnificent set of carved and painted Hampton Court-like state apartments on the second floor – it is also a Regency palace of the 6th Duke's. It survives as a remarkably complete and well-maintained expression of early-nineteenth-century taste, and a grandiose synthesis of Classical and Picturesque principles. Dr Waagen, the Prussian art historian and recorder of English art collections, who visited in the mid-nineteenth century, described Chatsworth as a 'princely residence' and considered it to be chiefly a monument to the 6th Duke's patronage.

The 6th Duke of Devonshire succeeded his father in 1811. He inherited the 1st Duke's house largely unaltered, apart from a subsidiary service wing added to the north in the mid-eighteenth century, by James Paine, and some remodelling of the south-front drawing rooms for the 5th Duke in the 1780s, by John Carr and François Hervé, a French decorator from the Carlton House stable.

At first, the 6th Duke intended to keep all this and merely to convert the Long Gallery into a fashionable library-living room, without the assistance of an architect, by removing some of the wall panels and inserting shelves. His love of splendour, however, got the better of him, and he soon embarked on a much more radical and ambitious scheme to provide an entirely new set of magnificent entertaining rooms, as well as more comfortable private rooms for

Above: Both the conservatory and the dominating Corinthian belvedere – the 'Temple Attic' – were additions to Wyatville's original designs of 1818–20, at the 6th Duke of Devonshire's behest. The Temple Attic is a spectacular demonstration of Picturesque aesthetics and was intended to enhance the landscape impact of Chatsworth in its setting.

Right: View from the Temple Attic showing the surrounding park landscaped for the 4th Duke by Capability Brown, and the distant Italianate outline of Froggett Edge and other Derbyshire hills.

Above: *Enfilade through the drawing rooms. The 6th Duke inserted pairs of double mahogany doors to 'open up' the rooms for entertaining.*

Right: *The sculpture gallery, photographed in 1994. 'A place that was to receive three of Canova's works … excited grand ideas.' The project for a sculpture gallery at Chatsworth was probably originally inspired by the Duke of Bedford's example at Woburn, but received a fillip when the 6th Duke visited Rome in 1819 and became besotted with marble.*

himself. In some ways, his reconstruction was similar to George IV's transformation of the interior of Windsor, but the Duke started earlier, and his suite of entertaining rooms was even grander and more varied, comprising a large library, vast dining room, sculpture gallery, conservatory and theatre, as well as three large drawing rooms, all in a consistent Classical style, notable for its restrained sumptuousness. The result is a model demonstration of the Regency idea of a great house.

His immediate inspiration may have been the 6th Duke of Bedford's creation of a sculpture gallery and a new 200-foot long greenhouse at Woburn. The Duke of Devonshire adopted the same architect, Jeffry Wyatt (to be called Wyatville throughout for ease of

Above: The tribune. Though comparatively small, this is Wyatville's most impressive and ingenious space at Chatsworth, and forms the link between the libraries and the new wing. Wyatville's design was admired as a 'kind of tribune he invented – keeping the central line, and yet not projecting offensively on the outside'. The four antique marble columns came from Richmond House and cost £50 each.

Left: The library. The Baroque Long Gallery was converted into a library-sitting room in line with Regency social conventions, and to house the Duke's superlative book collection. The cases were made in London by Armstrong & Siddon in 1826. The thick, rich carpet was specially woven for the room at Axminster and reflects Edward Goudge's seventeenth-century ceiling.

reference). But whereas the Bedford new works comprised a loosely linked, covered walk through the grounds, the Duke of Devonshire's were one magnificent axial enfilade continuing the *piano nobile* of the seventeenth-century house.

Wyatville was employed in January 1818 to survey the existing building and to produce for the Duke a 'general plan of improvements' to enable him 'by slow degrees to proceed with at such times as may suit him hereafter'. This was the overture to twenty years of constant building work. Though Wyatville was the architect, the enlargement and remodelling of Chatsworth was to an exceptional extent the Duke's personal hobby, and he supervised every detail, developed or deviated from the original plans, and expressed many of his own personal ideas and enthusiasms.

This was just as well, for though Wyatville was an excellent architectural planner and a thoroughly efficient project manager, he was an unimaginative and insensitive designer, and it required real input from the client to raise his work above the commonplace, as with George IV at Windsor. This was certainly true also of Chatsworth, and it is the 6th Duke's own sophisticated, international taste which makes the early-nineteenth-century work there so exciting and impressive. Wyatville, amenable and efficient, rose to the

occasion and planned a series of rooms to suit the Duke's princely style, as well as extending the building in a way that dramatically altered its external impact in the sublime landscape setting.

Wyatville suggested replacing Paine's offices with a new wing of palatial Classical architecture nearly 400 feet long, containing large entertaining rooms, extra bedrooms and a complete set of modern kitchen offices. He explained: 'These designs are formed on the principle of adhering to the character of the present building, of gaining all the required advantages and adding to the grandeur of the place.' Work started in 1820 and the structure was completed by 1824, though the interior fitting continued for many years after that.

Some of the most dramatic aspects of the project were introduced while work was in progress and were due to the Duke's personal interventions, including the addition of a large conservatory to the main suite of rooms, and a towering Corinthian belvedere at the northern extremity of the new wing. The Duke christened this the 'Temple Attic' and a neighbour, Lady Wharncliffe, 'the Poussin', hinting at the Picturesque source of inspiration for this unprecedented architectural feature in the Classical ruins depicted in the background of Seicento paintings.

The Temple Attic is the most prominent external feature of Chatsworth and the key to the whole of the Regency composition. The Duke got the idea, so he said in his *Handbook to Chatsworth and Hardwick*, at Oxford from 'the tower of the Schools which forms part of the Bodleian. Sir Jeffry had not intended to build anything above the ballroom but readily adopted my plan'. The belvedere accentuates the character of the new wing as a large asymmetrical addition, which is in itself as strong a feature in the landscape as the seventeenth-century main block. This assertive asymmetry was also an architectural idea of the Duke's. As he said: 'I admire an irregular room, if it is composed of regular parts and the same maxim is good for a house, and eminently so for Chatsworth.'

The antique marble columns used throughout the new rooms, the ormolu capitals of the sculpture gallery, the console brackets in the same room, based on some in the Vatican, and the white *scagliola* walls of the Small Dining Room (reminiscent of the Winter Palace in St Petersburg), all were the Duke's own choice and reflect his cosmopolitan taste and culture and the impact on him of Paris, Rome (which he first visited in 1819) and Russia (where he was Ambassador-Extraordinary from George IV at Tsar Nicholas I's Coronation in 1826).

Wyatville's alterations greatly enhanced the convenience and comfort of the house, with enclosed corridors on three sides of the original quadrangle, giving access to the Duke's own apartments, and

The dining room. It is like 'dining in a great trunk and you expect the lid to open …' wrote the Duke humorously of Wyatville's gilt segmental coffered ceiling. Yellow scagliola was first considered for the walls, but white marble was chosen for the dado. The two marble doorcases were framed by pairs of antique marble columns bought from the Duke of Richmond. The two chimneypieces are an original design, flanked by life-size Bacchic figures carved by R. W. Sievier and Richard Westmacott (Junior).

guest bedrooms on the north and west fronts. Further luxurious guest bedrooms and dressing rooms, hung with Chinese wallpaper, were made on the top floor of the east front, and smaller bachelor bedrooms included in the new north wing to the west of the grand rooms and, like them, approached by the new Oak Stairs.

The entertaining rooms comprised three drawing rooms along the south front, where the Duke richly augmented the existing architecture with ornamental plasterwork, new marble chimneypieces, silk and gilding. The library was thoroughly remodelled by Wyatville in 1824, with two tiers of bookshelves made in London by Armstrong & Siddon. A new chimneypiece was installed and a Baroque stucco cornice contrived by Bernasconi (who was chief stuccador at Chatsworth, as at Windsor, Buckingham Palace and Ashridge), with shells and scrolls to match Edward Goudge's ceiling – the only feature of the Baroque Long Gallery to be retained.

Beyond in the ante-library, Bernasconi modelled a new ceiling inspired by Goudge's in the main library. Beyond that again, in the new north wing, the tribune, dining room, music lobby and sculpture gallery marched in majestic succession, linked by pairs of double mahogany doors and resplendent with antique marble columns.

The sculpture gallery was the Duke's particular pride and joy: 'The contents of this room offered me great satisfaction and pleasure and are among the excuses for an extravagance that I can neither deny nor justify.' The Duke had spent much time visiting the studios of the international group of sculptors when he visited Rome in 1819, and commissioned works from his own countrymen, such as John Gibson, Campbell and R. J. Wyatt, as well as from Canova and Tenerani, Thorwaldsen and Schadow.

He considered lining the walls with marble but chose Derbyshire stone instead. Dr Waagen thought its 'warm yellow … relieves the white marble' of the statues. The doorcases at either end are framed by rare marble columns. Those at the south end were bought by the Duke at 'an obscure shop' in Paris and he commissioned the ormolu capitals from Delafontaine while there. Those at the north end were bought with Richard Westmacott's advice and the capitals made in Derbyshire 'at a fifth of the price'. Westmacott also advised on the marble plinths of the statues, which are of Cipollino, porphyry, granite and *fior di Persico*.

The conservatory leading out of the sculpture gallery was begun in 1826 and completed in 1828. The theatre-ballroom at the far end beneath the Temple Attic was only fitted out in the 1830s, ten years after the completion of the shell. By 1841, the 6th Duke had spent £260,956.16s.8d on his improvements, and by 1848, with Paxton's help, the total had reached £313,608.1s.5d. It was the most expensive private house project of the age.

The Yellow Drawing Room. The original family drawing room had been redecorated for the 6th Duke's parents by Carr of York and Hervé. The 6th Duke added rococo plasterwork to the ceiling and masses of gilding as well as hanging the walls with silk, to bring the room into line with the new entertaining rooms.

Above: *The Wellington Bedroom. The Prince Regent's work at Brighton Pavilion rekindled the contemporary taste for chinoiserie and many Regency bedrooms were hung with Chinese paper.*

Left: *The Alcove Bedroom. The 6th Duke contrived a whole series of new guest bedrooms on the upper floors at Chatsworth, which are the most extensive Regency series to survive. The original hangings are characteristic examples of the Regency taste for upholstery.*

⇜ ASHRIDGE PARK, HERTFORDSHIRE ⇝

Ashridge was the largest and grandest complete new-build among early-nineteenth-century English houses, so many of the others being reconstructions of existing buildings, as at Chatsworth and Windsor. Despite this, it is today little known or indeed admired, partly because it has been in institutional use since the 1920s, partly because early-nineteenth-century Gothic work is unfashionable. (Commissioners' Gothic churches of the same date and similar architecture, for instance, are today disregarded and regularly demolished throughout the industrial towns of the Midlands and the North.) Early-nineteenth-century Gothic Revival is thought to lack the charm of Georgian Gothick, on the one hand, and the originality of full-blown Victorian Gothic, on the other. It is serious, but not serious enough.

Even contemporaries were ambivalent about Ashridge. As Repton put it somewhat defensively in his Red Book: 'It may perhaps be asked by the fastidious Antiquary whether the whole Edifice most resembles a Castle, an Abbey or a Collegiate pile. To which may be given this simple answer: It is a modern House on a large scale, where the character of the rich Gothic of Henry VII has been successfully

introduced and imitated.' Pückler-Muskau gave the obvious retort when he said modern Gothic was 'just as ridiculous and incongruous, as if you were to meet the possessor of these pretty flower gardens walking about them in helm and harness.'

Ashridge is, however, a very impressive piece of architecture, both in its Picturesque composition and its spatial qualities, as well as being a magnificent display of virtuoso Regency craftsmanship in stonework, woodcarving and stucco decoration. The neatly elegant execution speaks of Georgian civilisation. There were strong historical associational reasons for choosing the Gothic style here, as the site had been a medieval college of Augustinian canons, of which some remains survived, including an ancient barn which at Repton's suggestion was incorporated in the garden layout. Nor was late-Perpendicular Gothic incompatible with the Regency domestic ideal,

Above: *The north front with James Wyatt's main block, staircase tower, service wing and chapel spire and Jeffry Wyatville's north porch and flanking buildings.*
Right: *The north porch.*

as the large areas of traceried glazing, canted bay windows and arched cloisters were all features suited to the early-nineteenth-century love of light, views and integral conservatory walks.

At Ashridge, as at Windsor, Gothic was chosen for the external architecture, the halls and staircases, as well as, of course, for the chapel, but the principal reception rooms were finished in Classical taste. This was the beginning of a decorative convention which lasted for over a hundred years where different styles were adopted for different interiors: Classical (French or Adams) being deemed appropriate for Victorian and Edwardian drawing rooms, and panelled Jacobethan or Gothic for halls, dining rooms or billiard rooms.

Above: *The staircase hall. The plaster fan vault was modelled by Francis Bernasconi. In the centre is a wind dial.*

Right: *The staircase. Designed by James Wyatt (completed by Benjamin Dean Wyatt). It rises the full height of the central tower, a spatial impact comparable to Fonthill – four lofty storeys. Pückler-Muskau described it as 'the most magnificent of its kind that can be imagined'. The walls are faced in ashlar stone and the rails are of polished brass. The statues in niches of the Kings of England associated with Ashridge are by Richard Westmacott (Junior).*

Left: *The hall. The exaggerated scale bespeaks late-Georgian Romanticism, but the hammerbeam roof is a scholarly job in the spirit of that of the hall at Christ Church, Oxford. The 'antique' furniture – benches and tables – was designed by Benjamin Dean Wyatt. Antlers and heraldry complete the effect.*

Ashridge was designed by James Wyatt and was completed after his death by his son Benjamin Dean Wyatt and his nephew Jeffry (Wyatville), both of whom had been his assistants on the project. It is James Wyatt's most serious Gothic building and shows of what he was capable when 'invested with almost unlimited powers and funds'. The large main block, square and solid, is connected by a long lower wing to the chapel whose prickly spire forms a soaring asymmetrical counterbalance. It is a Gothic version of the same Picturesque architectural composition as the 6th Duke of Devonshire's Chatsworth. While the entrance front is severely reticent, almost fortified in appearance, the garden front is suitably domestic, with large canted bays and oriels and a more cheerful and open character. The halls, staircase and chapel are spectacular concepts by any standards, and are the English Gothic equivalent of the Baroque spaces of German eighteenth-century princely palaces. They aspire to the sublime.

The kitchen. With its great hooded stone fireplace, high open roof and simpler architectural character, this two-storeyed room was the most convincing Gothic interior at Ashridge.

Above: *The library. The principal living rooms were fitted out in a simpler Classical style.*

Right: *The chapel. The architecture was designed by James Wyatt and the fittings by Jeffry Wyatville. The choir stalls and organ case were carved in a remarkably convincing Gothic manner by Edward Wyatt. The individual tabernacled stalls on the return walls were the throne-like seats of Lord and Lady Bridgewater.*

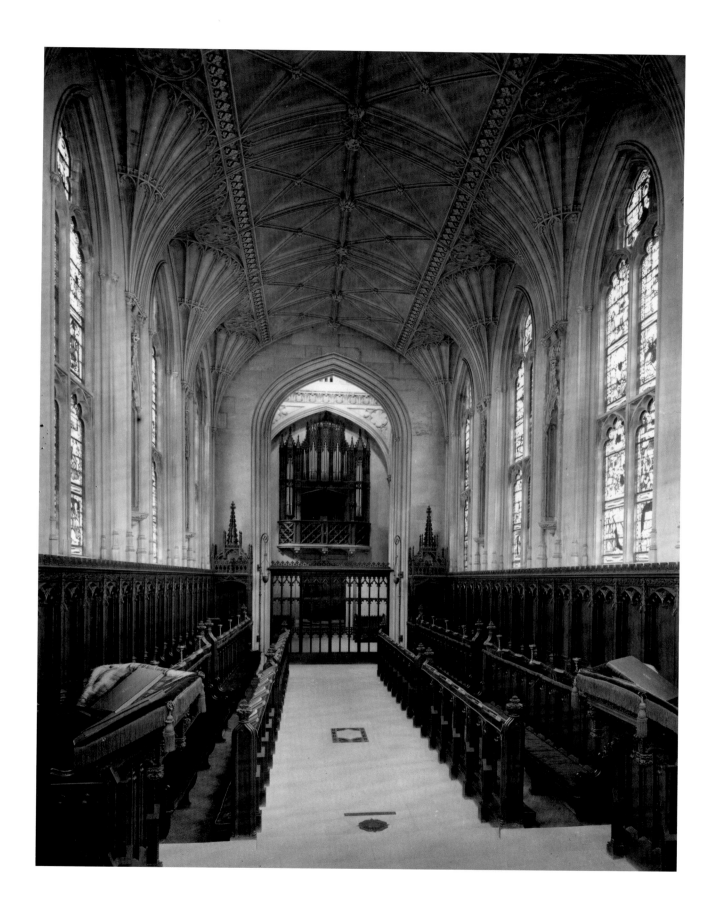

The Ashridge estate was inherited, together with a vast fortune, from the 3rd Duke of Bridgewater in 1803 by John Egerton, a distant cousin and son of the Bishop of Durham who descended from a younger brother of the 1st Duke. Though the dukedom had become extinct, he succeeded to the older earldom, which had been created in 1617 for the son of Lord Chancellor Thomas Egerton, Viscount Brackley. The 3rd Duke was the famous 'Canal Duke', a hero of the Industrial Revolution who had ventured his whole capital on creating a system of inland waterways, working with James Brindley, the engineer. He was triumphantly successful in the end, and the Bridgewater Canal from Worsley to Manchester halved the price of coal in the latter place while bringing the Duke the staggering income of £110,000 per annum.

On his death in 1803, he divided his fortune between two cousins: Worsley, Ellesmere, the London house and his picture collection went to the second son of the Duke of Sutherland (created Earl of Ellesmere); Ashridge and the estates in the South, together with an income of £70,000 per annum, went to the 7th Earl of Bridgewater. The Canal Duke had demolished the old house at Ashridge and never got round to building a new one. He had camped out there in a plain little brick box like a rectory. Lord Bridgewater immediately celebrated his good fortune by planning a new house on a palatial scale. The choice of Tudor Gothic reflected the monastic origins of the place and also its royal connections, for after the Dissolution it had become a royal property and Elizabeth I had lived there during the reign of Queen Mary. The Lord Chancellor had bought it from James I in 1604. The foundation stone was laid by Charlotte Catherine Anne, Countess of Bridgewater, on 25 October 1808, as commemorated by a brass plate in the hall, and Wyatt's shell – constructed in ashlar stone, not brick and stucco – rose rapidly.

After James Wyatt's death in 1813, Jeffry Wyatville completed the design, adding the north entrance porch in 1816, a conservatory and irregular asymmetrical flanking wings, one for stables, the other for smaller private family rooms, which increased the overall composition to over 600 feet long, enhancing the picturesque appearance. He also designed the fittings for James Wyatt's chapel, just as Benjamin Dean finished the staircase and designed the Gothic furniture for the halls. Edward Wyatt was responsible for the excellent woodcarving, while Bernasconi did the plasterwork. Richard Westmacott (Junior) was the sculptor providing chimneypieces and royal statues, including one of Queen Elizabeth I.

As completed in 1818, Ashridge is one of the grandest monuments of Regency Romantic taste. *Country Life* photographed Ashridge twice before its sale and conversion in the 1920s and these early-twentieth-century photographs are a unique record of the house when it was still in private hands, fully furnished and its gardens immaculately maintained. Sadly, Ashridge is one of the few major Regency houses not still privately lived in and where the family is extinct.

The garden front, showing Jeffry Wyatville's conservatory screening the subsidiary office wing.

BELVOIR CASTLE, LEICESTERSHIRE

The best contemporary description of Belvoir in the 5th Duke of Rutland's lifetime is by Charles Greville. He recorded that the family lived there for three or four months a year from October to March, including Christmas and for the celebration of the Duke's birthday in January. Even to Greville, who knew George IV's Windsor and was accustomed to the greatest houses, Belvoir seemed an establishment 'kept up with extraordinary splendour'.

He described a typical winter house party: 'In the morning we are roused by the strains of martial music and the band [of his regiment of militia] marches round the terrace, awakening or quickening the guests with lively airs. All the men hunt or shoot. At dinner there is a different display of plate every day and in the evening some play at whist or amuse themselves as they please, and some walk about the staircases and corridors to hear the band which plays the whole evening in the hall. On the Duke's birthday there was a great feast in the castle. Two hundred people dined in the servants' hall alone, without considering the other tables. We were about forty at dinner. When the cloth was removed, Esterhazy proposed

The north and west fronts with Thoroton's porte-cochère marking the main entrance on the left and Wyatt's Regent's Tower and chapel turrets.

Left and below: *The entrance hall and processional spaces at Belvoir were designed in the Gothic style by the Revd Sir John Thoroton, the ducal chaplain and an amateur architect, after the 1816 fire. The weapons are from the Duke's militia.*

His Grace's health, who has always a speech prepared in which he returns thanks.'

The moving force behind the Regency reconstruction of Belvoir and the incredible neo-feudal *vie de château* maintained there was not the Duke, however, but his forceful wife Elizabeth. Born a Howard of Castle Howard, on marrying the Duke she had found the seventeenth-century castle, a dumpy Classical edifice designed by John Webb on the Norman foundations, much below her expectations and unworthy of its spectacular hilltop site with wide views over six counties, towards the distant silhouette of Lincoln Cathedral and the far, silver line of the North Sea, 40 miles away. She called in James Wyatt in 1800 to make it into the castle it ought to have been. The result, completed in 1823, was in Christopher Hussey's phrase, 'the apotheosis of Regency taste'. Mrs Arbuthnot, the Duke of Wellington's friend, stated in her diary in 1823: 'The castle has been built ... by the present Duchess who has made the place, the Duke taking no part in the improvement.'

The reconstruction began in earnest with the demolition of the 1660s south front on Good Friday 1801. The new house was to be a feudal Gothic palace with magnificent views outwards and towards the castle itself. The south and west fronts containing new family apartments and a chapel were rapidly constructed of brilliant yellow ironstone with silvery stone dressings, creating a richly Picturesque effect. In 1803, the round tower was begun and later named after the Prince Regent, who visited Belvoir in 1814 with his brother the Duke of York, a very close friend of the Duchess of Rutland. Wyatt's interiors, including the Regent's Gallery (the tower formed its bow window) were Classical, as was often the case inside Regency Gothic shells.

In October 1816, a fire broke out, and the north and east sides of the castle were destroyed, the flames only being halted by bricking up the entrance to the Regent's Gallery. The 'whole of the old part of the Castle' was lost, according to the Duchess, along with the newly built staircase, entrance hall and picture gallery (and a third of the art collection). Undaunted (the house had been insured), the Duchess began rebuilding the lost sections in March 1817 in an even more Picturesquely Flamboyant Gothic manner, using the Duke's chaplain, the Revd Sir John Thoroton (whose mother was the 3rd Duke's illegitimate daughter), as architect, James Wyatt himself having died in 1813.

A Flamboyant Gothic porte-cochère was added to the north entrance front, and a new bowed tower built on the east side to contain a large drawing room or ballroom and improve the silhouette. The existing Staunton Tower was also heightened, to match James Wyatt's south tower containing the Duchess's apartments. Inside, the new hall, galleries and staircases were all Gothic with pointed arches and plaster vaults forming a Picturesque procession of inter-related spaces. The piecemeal rebuilding and the amateur nature of Thoroton's and the Duchess's direction created defects of practical planning, as both Greville and Mrs Arbuthnot noticed. The latter stated the castle had 'great faults' as there was 'no regular suite of rooms' opening directly into each other in the preferred Regency manner.

The Duchess also called on James Wyatt's sons, Benjamin Dean and Philip, to design the principal new interiors, including the top-lit picture gallery and the principal dining room in an impressively monumental Roman style. Cousin Edward Wyatt was also employed for carving and gilding. Suites of guest bedrooms were given characteristic Wyatt acanthus cornices and hung with fashionable Chinese wallpaper and painted silk. Belvoir, therefore, had a much wider range of interiors than most Regency houses, and is a veritable showcase of Regency styles. This was emphasised by the novel and dazzling decoration of the principal drawing room – named the Elizabeth Saloon in the Duchess's memory after her sudden death from appendicitis in 1825.

The Elizabeth Saloon was designed for the Duchess by Matthew Cotes Wyatt, James Wyatt's younger son, who was more of a decorative painter and sculptor than an architect, and this may explain its theatrical, scenic character. The Duchess chose the 'Louis Quatorze' style for the room, making it the first complete interior in a style that was made ultra-fashionable by the Wyatts' Crockford's Club in St James's, opened in 1827. It was to remain a staple theme for rich drawing rooms for a hundred years. M. C. Wyatt bought genuine French boiseries for the walls in Paris as a job lot for 1,450 guineas. These actually dated from the 1730s, the reign of Louis XV, but the 'Louis Quatorze' style was a generalised hybrid, a tribute to Versailles and *ancien régime* French taste rather than a strictly chronological designation.

Above: *The entrance porch.*

Right: *The Regent's Gallery, fitted up and furnished for the Prince Regent's stay in 1814. The Gobelin tapestries from the Don Quixote series woven in the 1760s to designs by Coypel, and some Boulle furniture, were bought by the Duke and Duchess in Paris on a visit in 1814.*

The carpet was specially woven for the room in Tournai in the
French Savonnerie manner, incorporating the Rutland peacock crest.
The ceiling was painted by Matthew Cotes Wyatt himself, incorporating portraits of the Duke and Duchess of Rutland and the Duke of
York in mythological guises as Juno, Jupiter and the King of the
Gods. The Duchess's avowed aim was to create 'a Blaze of
Splendour'. The room had the desired effect. Mrs Arbuthnot
described it as 'the most magnificent room I ever saw, fitted up in the
style of Louis 14th in pannells of blue silk damask and the most
beautiful carving and gilding'. After Elizabeth's death, the discon-
solate Duke placed a life-size white marble statue, sculpted by
Matthew Cotes Wyatt, as a memorial in front of a large looking glass.

Above: *The dining room was designed by Benjamin Dean and Philip Wyatt in a severe
Roman style with marmoreal pilasters typical of Regency dining rooms. Forty guests
regularly sat down to dinner during the 5th Duke's winter house parties. The monumental
sideboards, typical of bespoke Regency dining-room furniture, were supplied by Gillow, as
was much of the furniture at Belvoir.*

Right: *A marble pedestal in the dining room, carved by M. C. Wyatt with a trompe l'œil
white marble cloth and showing Regency taste at its most Baroque.*

Left: *The Elizabeth Saloon. This 'Blaze of Splendour' was designed by M. C. Wyatt with
genuine 1730s French boiseries framing blue silk on the walls. It is the earliest example of
the Louis XIV interior, which became another popular strand in the Regency stylistic galaxy.*

Above: *The Duchess of Rutland walking eternally into her creation.*
Life-size marble statue carved by M. C. Wyatt after her sudden death in 1825.

Right: *The Duchess's Bedroom.*

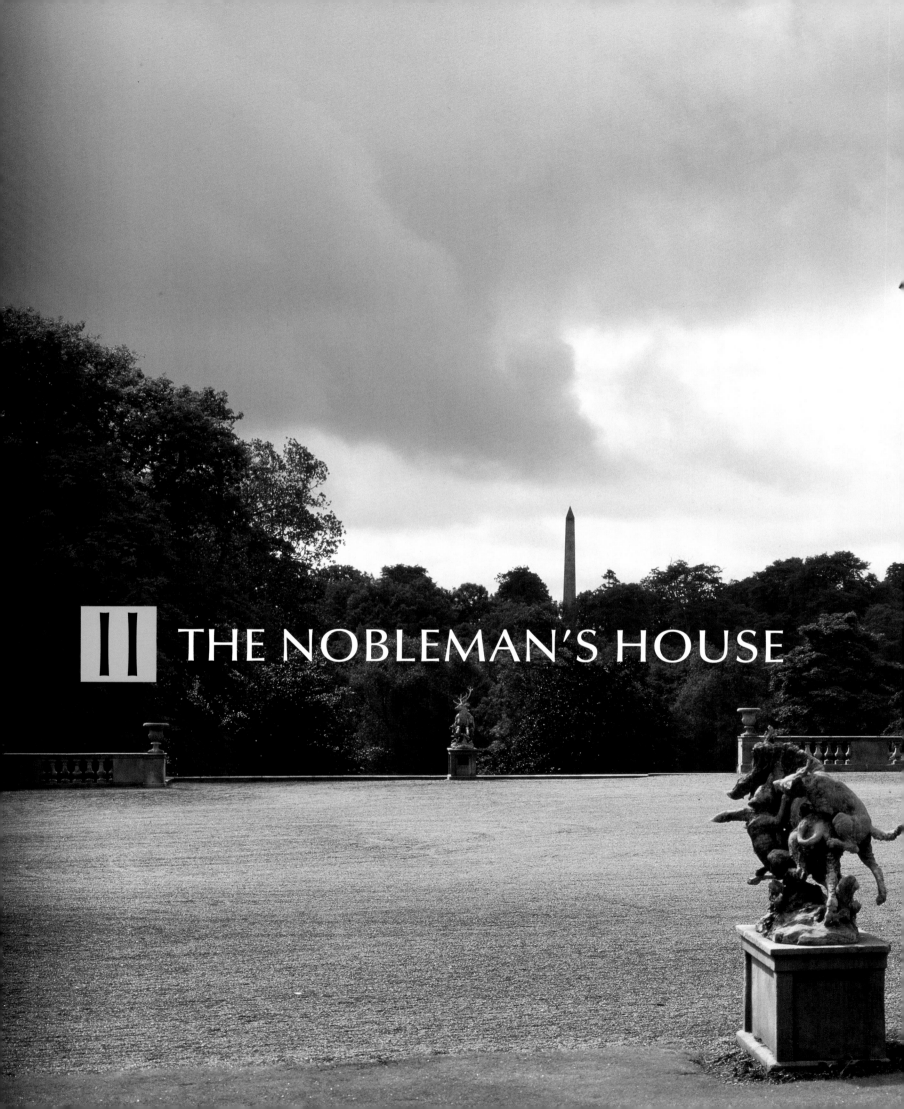

II THE NOBLEMAN'S HOUSE

IVIDING Regency country houses into the nobleman's and the gentleman's houses is an artificial exercise, but it reflects to some degree contemporary thought and is more than a matter of scale, though the former of course tend to be larger than the latter. With the great expansion of the British economy in the second half of the eighteenth century, the creation of many new fortunes, and the influx of new families setting up as landed gentry, acquiring estates and buying, remodelling or building country houses, many established noble families wished to keep ahead of the game and express their more distinguished lineage and superior rank in architectural terms. This they did partly through the lavish smartness of their interiors but also by stressing the antiquity of their seats and building castles or Tudor Gothic houses.

The Regency saw the beginning of the idea of the country house as a distinctive architectural genre, an idea which became widespread in the mid-nineteenth century. It was only in the late 1830s and 1840s that 'Jacobethan' and Gothic began to be considered as the country house style *par excellence* in the hands of Salvin, Blore, Wyatt and Brandon, William Burn and other prolific early Victorian architects, while Classical was an essentially urban style. But the stirrings of this architectural outlook can be detected in the first decades of the nineteenth century and is represented to an extent by George IV with Gothic at Windsor and Classical in London. The Earl of Lonsdale and Earl Somers, both Tory grandees, commissioned Smirke to build castles as being commensurate with their neo-feudal noble outlook.

Wilkins, the Bucklers, Donthorne and other architects evolved Regency brands of Tudor Revival which seemed particularly appropriate for large country houses. They expressed the Picturesque, as well as social, theories first promoted by Uvedale Price and Payne Knight, who had extolled the castle and Tudor styles in the late eighteenth century as being especially fitting for the rural landscape. An aspect of this Regency artistic outlook was the beginning of the great nineteenth-century heraldic revival, which reached a climax in Pugin's decoration of the Palace of Westminster. Thomas Willement and J. C. Buckler, however, were already devising the most thorough-going armorial decoration in the 1820s, at Windsor Castle, Costessey Hall in Norfolk and elsewhere, including heraldic carpets as well as more obvious displays like stained glass and carved and painted friezes. The new-rich soon jumped on to all these bandwagons, but that does not mean that there was not a Regency idea of a suitable scale and form of architectural expression for a nobleman's house.

There was a certain political tincture to Regency taste. Those nobles who veered towards castles and 'Tudor' were often the Tories. The grand Whiggery, rich and cosmopolitan, tended to stick to Classical. Graeco-Roman still spoke of a liberal education and familiarity with the literature and art of the Ancients, as well as of the mainstream European artistic canon. Fastidious designers like C. R. Cockerell or learned amateurs like Sir Charles Monck (Middleton) considered scholarly Classicism to be the highest form of architectural expression.

In defining 'nobles', it seemed best to follow nineteenth-century custom and usage and include Irish peers, as well as the strict English and United Kingdom peerage, and also the heads of families where the builder himself may not have been titled (thanks to side-ways inheritance) but where predecessors and successors were, as with the Pennants of Penrhyn Castle.

EASTNOR CASTLE, HEREFORDSHIRE Above: *The austerity of the architecture is offset by the beauty of the contrived landscape with wooded slopes, a lake and glimpses of the Malvern Hills in the background. The house sits on a castellated terrace.*

ICKWORTH, SUFFOLK Left: *Corridor linking the rotunda and the wing.*

WYNYARD PARK, COUNTY DURHAM Preceding pages: *The entrance front designed by Philip Wyatt for the 3rd Marquess and Marchioness of Londonderry.*

≽ EATON HALL, CHESHIRE ≼

The Grosvenors recorded their direct male line descent from Robert
le Grosvenor of Budworth in Cheshire, who had received his lands in
a grant from the Earl of Chester in 1160, making them one of the
small group of English families who could trace their holdings back to
the pattern of sub-infeudation after the Norman Conquest. Created
baronets by James I in 1622, their rise had been rapid in the eighteenth century thanks to marriage to heiresses and the supremely
successful development of their Mayfair estate in London and mines
in Flintshire.

Richard Grosvenor's father had been created an earl by George III
in 1784. He himself was to be advanced to a marquessate in William

IV's Coronation Honours in 1831. As 2nd Earl Grosvenor, he was
both of ancient descent and very rich indeed. He inherited at Eaton a
compact Restoration double pile, red-brick house designed by
William Samwell. This had been suitable for his baronet ancestors but
was not good enough for him. As soon as he inherited in 1802, he set
about reconstructing it as a large Tudor Gothic house appropriate to
his lineage, his rank and his fortune.

His architect was William Porden, a pupil of James Wyatt's – as
were so many Regency architects. After a stint in the 22nd Dragoons,
a regiment raised by Lord Sheffield, one of Wyatt's clients, Porden
returned to architecture in the 1780s and was lucky enough to be
appointed surveyor to the Grosvenor Estate, by the 1st Earl
Grosvenor. Presumably his military bearing inspired confidence.
Through the Grosvenor connection he built up a large country house
practice and, as has been seen, got the large commission for the
stables at Brighton from the Prince Regent in 1804, at Lord
Grosvenor's recommendation.

*Above: The drawing room. This was in one of the lower flankers that Porden added to
Samwell's house, with a bay window facing east over the garden to the River Dee.
The splendid fan-vaulted ceiling also contains shields of arms.*

*Left: The saloon. This occupied the centre of the garden front on the site of Samwell's
saloon. The centre of the ceiling had richly modelled plasterwork surrounded by a fan vault
by Bernasconi.*

Eaton Hall for the 2nd Earl Grosvenor was, however, his major architectural commission and was considered 'the most extravagant Gothic house of the Regency period'. The shell of Samwell's house was retained in the centre and flanked by larger-scaled new rooms, and totally encased in elaborate Gothic dress derived in spirit from Henry VII's Chapel, Westminster. The construction made lavish use of cast iron for window tracery and balustrade quatrefoils to create the most frilly and prickly effect possible. Coade stone was also used for details and statues. Building on site took from 1804 to 1812.

Then Lord Grosvenor had another go in the 1820s, adding outer flanking wings designed by Benjamin Gummow, a local Welsh architect who had supervised the construction on site of Porden's designs and had stayed on as salaried surveyor to Lord Grosvenor's Flintshire and Cheshire estates, designing or executing subsidiary buildings there.

Porden had no very high opinion of his assistant, telling Lord Grosvenor that Gummow was a man who 'speaks without thinking and is the most inconsistent man I ever met with'. Nevertheless, his 1820 additions to Eaton were competently Pordenesque in spirit and, in engravings, were indistinguishable from his master's work.

The interior of Eaton was as fantastically Gothic as the exterior, with endless plaster fan vaulting and vast traceried windows full of heraldic stained glass in the upper lights. The bottom panes were large sheets of plate glass to take advantage of the views. The use of this technically advanced product, like the cast-iron tracery and Coade ornament, shows Porden's progressive combination of the Gothic style with up-to-date industrial processes, but must have given Eaton something of a mass-produced or manufactured feel despite the vast cost. Over £100,000 had been spent by 1812.

Eaton was distinctively Regency, reinforced by the degree to which the interior was the work of interior decorators rather than its architects and relied for its main effects on 'upholstery', brightly coloured and co-ordinated hangings, curtains and carpets, rather than specifically architectural effects. The furnishing contract was given to Gillow of Lancaster, whose London showroom was on the Grosvenor Estate in Mayfair and in any case enjoyed a near monopoly of furnishing houses in the North West during the Regency period. For Eaton, Gillow's adapted their usual forms to Gothic to suit the architecture, with crockets and tracery executed in mahogany and exotic woods with brass inlays and mounts.

Pückler-Muskau, who was not thrilled by Eaton, described them as 'shapeless tables and chairs, which most incongruously affected to imitate architectural ornaments'. The decoration itself was done by Porden's son-in-law Joseph Kay, who chose the colours – lashings of crimson – and draped the curtains. He 'understands them both as painter and upholsterer'. All the rooms had fitted carpets with overall patterns, another Regency preference, and hearth rugs *en suite*, matching the general colour scheme of the room, which was different in each case.

The array of elaborate Tudor Gothic at Eaton was specifically chosen as the most suitable for a nobleman's house. Porden advocated Gothic to his client as 'preserving that distinction to rank and

Fortune which it is the habit of the age to diminish ... with regard to splendour it is far superior [to classical], and its variety is infinite', and, therefore, of course, expensive.

William Porden may have emphasised the feudal undertones of Gothic, but to many visitors, Eaton reeked of only one thing – money. Pückler-Muskau with his usual clear perception described it as a 'chaos of modern gothic excrescences' and went on to add: 'All the magnificence lay in the gorgeous materials, and the profuse display of money'.

Regency Eaton only lasted a generation. It was remodelled and made more serious and less of a 'gothic Brighton Pavilion' by William Burn in the 1840s, totally reconstructed by Alfred Waterhouse in the 1870s, demolished in 1963, and has been twice rebuilt or reconstructed since then.

Porden's, Gummow's, Gillow's and Kay's interiors, however, were beautifully recorded in watercolours by John and J. C. Buckler and published by them in 1826. *Views of Eaton Hall, Cheshire* was a book which found a cult following, like Pyne's *Royal Residences* or Nash's *Views of the Royal Pavilion*, as part of the Regency Revival of the 1930s.

Above: The dining room. The walls, fitted carpet and curtains are all scarlet. The plaster vault is washed blue. A plain practical drugget covers the centre of the carpet. The table is shown in use for breakfast, a rare depiction. The Gillow furniture includes a typical Regency sideboard with mirror, to reflect and multiply the plate.

Left: The library. The Gillow furniture included the standard sofa tables, all overlaid with Gothic details and filigree. Several examples survive to demonstrate the quality and charm, rather than the incongruity of the treatment. The Buckler watercolours of Eaton Hall were published in Country Life *in 1971, when the magazine first started to use colour illustrations on a regular basis.*

Charles Somers Cocks, 2nd Lord Somers, was a characteristic Regency 'magnifico' and was raised to an earldom in the Coronation Honours of George IV in 1821. He was descended from Mary Somers, the sister and co-heir of Lord Chancellor Somers, a clever lawyer who had played a significant part in the Glorious Revolution of 1688, the Act of Union in 1706 and the succession of the Hanoverian dynasty in 1715 and was made Lord Somers (of the 1st creation). Charles inherited in 1806 and at first continued the Whig tradition of his family, but finally became a Tory in 1832 in opposition to the Great Reform Bill. He was a friend of the Duke of Wellington, under whom his eldest son served as an officer in the Peninsular War and was killed at the siege of Burgos in 1812. He is commemorated by an obelisk in the park at Eastnor.

Left: *View from across the lake. Although a compact, symmetrical rectangle, Smirke's design composes well from a distance with the four corner turrets, central raised tower and castellated chimneys making a bold silhouette and Picturesque composition.*

Below: *The staircase hall. A characteristic Regency Imperial plan with two branching arms leading to the bedrooms. The balustrade repeats that at Lowther Castle, now destroyed.*

These military connections and reactionary political views may perhaps partly explain Lord Somers's choice of the castle style when he came to build a new seat at Eastnor between 1812 and 1820. His choice of architect suggests as much. Robert Smirke was – in Howard Colvin's words – 'the favoured architect of the Tory establishment. It was to Tory patronage that he was indebted for all his official posts and for most of his commissions. His first major country house had been Lowther Castle for Lord Lonsdale, a Tory magnate'. Smirke enlarged or built thirty country houses, many of them castellated like Wilton Castle, Yorkshire, or Tudor as at Edmond Castle, in Cumberland, in contrast to his public works, which were purely Grecian and mainly Ionic.

The commission for Eastnor came in 1812, and building work carried on until 1820. The general concept was inspired by the central block of Smirke's previous work at Lowther (1806–11) and now that the latter is just a shell, Eastnor is the best surviving example of Smirke's castle houses. It is more compact than Lowther, without the latter's wide-spreading side wings. The symmetrical rectangular main block has quatrefoil-shaped towers at the four corners and a taller

central tower which forms the clerestory of the Great Hall below, a room 60 feet long and 60 feet high. The chimneys, too, are treated as castellated turrets to enliven the skyline. The outworks, including stables, gatehouse and terraces, are also castellated, enhancing the fortified feel of the place. All this feudalism was paid for by building development in a new London suburb – Somers Town, behind King's Cross Station.

Unlike Lowther with its pretty Perpendicular detailing, Eastnor is austerely treated in a mixture of Norman and early Gothic. Norman was another Regency stylistic preference, as demonstrated in the 11th Duke of Norfolk's Arundel Castle (1800–1815) where it was combined with Perpendicular, and at Belvoir (*see pages 74–81*) where it was one of the myriad styles displayed, and above all in Thomas Hopper's Penrhyn Castle (*see pages 94–9*). Regency Neo-Norman may sometimes seem rather prison-like, but at Eastnor the austerity of the architecture is offset by the boldness of the silhouette and the beauty of the Picturesque park setting, with wooded hills framing the views, a large artificial lake down below the terraces, and Claudian glimpses of the Malvern Hills.

As at Lowther, Smirke was structurally progressive, and the roof trusses at Eastnor are of cast iron. Another 'modern' feature is the large projecting porte-cochère. The plan is logically arranged around the central top-lit hall, with the imperial-plan staircase in a separate enclosure to one side. Both these dramatic spaces were only inhabitable because of a Regency form of central heating. The principal rooms included an octagonal saloon projecting into a canted bay in the centre of the garden front, and a large library, dining and drawing rooms on either side. As originally designed by Smirke for the 1st Earl, these were all rather plain rooms, relying for their effect on strong colours and appropriate displays of armour and portraits. All the main rooms, however, were considerably enriched and redecorated later in the nineteenth century, in the High Victorian manner.

Above: *The dining room. The original architecture has now been enhanced by the present owner's revival of strong colouring and a denser hang of family portraits.*

Right: *The drawing-room ceiling. The Regency architecture was overlain in the 1850s with A. W. N. Pugin's decorations, including coloured stencilling, heraldry, a Gothic chimneypiece and a large brass chandelier, inspired by one from Nuremberg, shown at the Great Exhibition in 1851. The plaster fan vault is characteristic work by Bernasconi.*

Penrhyn Castle is an example of the Regency country house at its most sublime and consistent. Everything about it is 'Norman', including some of the furniture, and it is the masterpiece of the architect Thomas Hopper, who first sprang to fashionable notice with his cast-iron conservatory for the Prince Regent at Carlton House. Penrhyn is characteristically Regency in that it is both a Picturesque celebration of magnificent landscape scenery and of British industrial, commercial and trading achievement. It enhances a beautiful site between the Menai Straits and the mountains of Snowdonia, while it was also a product of heroic entrepreneurial wealth and newly developed industrial techniques.

George Hay Dawkins Pennant, who built the castle from 1827 onwards, was the great-nephew of the 1st Lord Penrhyn, Richard Pennant, a Liverpool merchant and entrepreneurial genius who had married Anne Warburton, co-heiress of the Penrhyn estate. Richard Pennant used the fortune from his slave and sugar estates in Jamaica, Liverpool trading and salt mines in Cheshire to transform his wife's Welsh estate. What had been a remote and backward corner of Britain became one of the most admired wonders of the Industrial

Revolution, and a set-piece of 'modern improvement'. He expanded the small-scale quarrying in the Nant Ffrancon valley into a large-scale capitalist business, employing hundreds of men and exporting the slate to London and the world via a new road, an iron railway 6 miles long, and a new harbour: Port Penrhyn.

In the 1770s, London was still roofed in red tiles. Lord Penrhyn embarked on slate production in 1780. By 1800, London was largely a city of Welsh slate. By 1792, the Penrhyn quarries were exporting 12,000 tons of slate a year. The labourers were provided with model cottages, an inn and a hospital for the injured (quarrying slate was a dangerous business). Modern machinery was used where possible, including cranes and trains.

Pückler-Muskau, who visited in July 1828, was astounded by the

Right: *The hall looks like a section of Durham Cathedral, or perhaps a Schinkel stage set for a romantic opera. The candelabra with bronze Colza oil lamps were designed by Hopper and are 8 feet high. The stained glass inserted in the windows in the 1830s is by Thomas Willement, with signs of the zodiac and interlacing Celtic patterns.*

Below: *Thomas Hopper's Picturesque achievement and the stupendous scale of the house is captured in this colour photograph.*

'fearfully magnificent scene of operations' which was the deepest working in Europe in the early nineteenth century: 'It was like a subterranean World! Above the blasted walls of slate, smooth as a mirror and several hundred feet high, scarcely enough of the blue heaven was visible to enable me to distinguish mid-day from twilight … five or six high terraces of great extent rise one above another on the side of the mountain; along these swarm men, machines, trains of an hundred wagons attached together and rolling rapidly along iron railways …'.

Lord Penrhyn's agent, who planned, designed and managed this Celtic slate empire, was Benjamin Wyatt II, younger brother of the architects James and Samuel Wyatt. The latter designed a somewhat meagre new Gothic castle for Lord Penrhyn, built of white brick from Holkham in Norfolk (sent back as ballast in empty slate ships).

Compared to the sublime and awful spectacle of the quarry, the mountains and the sea, Samuel Wyatt's neat little Georgian 'castle' was a letdown. Dawkins Pennant lost no time after inheriting in embarking on a massive rebuilding to create a real castle, using Mona marble from the Isle of Anglesey, shipped across the Straits to the slate harbour at Port Penrhyn. The craftsmen employed to work the materials were also Dawkins Pennant's own men from the quarry, and the precision of the masonry owes much to their training and experience in splitting and dressing slate, as do virtuoso sidetables and other items of furniture carved out of slate itself.

As architecture, Hopper's Penrhyn trumps Smirke's Eastnor both in the scale and massing of the overall composition, but also in the astonishingly scholarly details, elaboration and variety of the Norman ornament deployed. The main block of Penrhyn, containing the Great

Hall, dining room, breakfast room, drawing room, and library-billiard room, is no bigger than that at Eastnor, and like the latter is entered through a Norman porte-cochère. Penrhyn, however, is flanked by dramatic subsidiary wings containing the service rooms and kitchens, yards and courts, stables and outbuildings, to form asymmetrical recessions of curtain walling, towers and turrets seemingly of infinite extent – actually, the length of two cricket fields laid end to end.

Beyond the main block rises a convincing square Norman tower 'keep', after the model of Rochester Castle. This contains the

Above: *The drawing room occupies the site, and represents the scale, of the Great Hall of the original medieval house. This had been associated with the Tudors, a historical resonance which may have affected the choice of an archaic style, although Hopper's principal aesthetic motivation was the Picturesque. The stencilled decoration, with stars on the ceiling, has been restored by the National Trust.*

Left: *The library-billiard room. In its function, this is the most typically Regency room in the house, used as a general, comfortable day-time living room. It is divided by 'Norman' arches into three sections, creating exciting spatial effects as well as preventing any sense of too daunting a scale. One section has the billiard table, here of course made of slate. Special provision for billiards in houses was another Regency innovation. Having assumed its modern form c. 1800, the game remained popular in country houses throughout the nineteenth century. There are four Mona marble chimneypieces, and heraldic decoration in the ceiling stucco. The window glass is by Willement.*

principal guest bedrooms (occupied by Queen Victoria and the Prince Consort in 1856), but provides the dramatic Perpendicular accent, which was the *sine qua non* of Regency Picturesque architectural planning. The counter-balance of the keep and the lower crenellated office wings roots Penrhyn into its magnificent setting – the sea in front, the mountains behind – and gives it the cyclopic scale and scenic drama necessary to hold its own in the landscape. A contemporary traveller described it as 'stately, massive and stupendous'.

The interior of Penrhyn is equally scenic, with vaulted passages, a hall like a section of the nave from a Norman cathedral, and an astonishing staircase where Celtic writhing beasts and accurately derived Norman mouldings and arches create a rising crescendo of Moorish extravagance culminating in a towering octagonal skylight. The principal rooms are equally consistently Norman, with chevron-patterned columns, cushion capitals and zigzag or billet moulded arches, all in carved wood or plaster by Bernasconi, and specially designed oak furniture in the Norman taste, described by one guest as 'exceedingly curious'.

Despite their scale, and the seemingly unpromising nature of 'Norman', the main rooms and bedrooms are pleasingly domestic,

with large round-headed windows, and sublime views out; and the warmth of hot-air central heating or patent grates and other Regency 'mod-cons' within. Hopper designed special bronze lamps and candelabra, originally fed by Colza oil, such as those 8 feet high and incorporating horses' heads in the Great Hall.

It may sound incredible, but those who knew the house when it was still lived in before the Second World War say that Penrhyn was a comfortable and pleasant place to stay: the rooms all close-carpeted and filled with small trees or large scented flowering shrubs in tubs (a form of appropriately scaled pot plants) and cheerful, blazing fires in all the grates, many of the rooms having two or three, or in the case of the library, four fireplaces.

Above: The breakfast room. A special, smaller eating room for breakfast – separate from the dining room – was one of the innovations of Regency house planning. The coffered 'Norman' ceiling is a virtuoso display of plasterwork by Bernasconi.

Left: The dining room. The massive fireplace is made of slate, the source of the wealth which paid for the house. The stencilled decoration was accurately restored by the National Trust in the 1980s.

Right: The staircase. This rising crescendo of beak head ornament, interlacing arches and writhing Celtic patterns is Hopper's most exciting and original space at Penrhyn. The stucco is by Bernasconi. The small Norman arches on the plaster vault are particularly enjoyable, and there is dramatic top lighting from an octagonal skylight.

≽ TREGOTHNAN, CORNWALL ≼

The Regency period saw the beginning of the rise of the Tudor or 'Jacobethan' style as the preferred stylistic dish for English country houses, a fashion which predominated in the 1830s and 1840s, and lasted until the end of the nineteenth century, and beyond, when it was overtaken by the twentieth-century Neo-Georgian Revival. Tregothnan, designed by William Wilkins in 1816 for the 1st Earl of Falmouth, is one of the earliest and finest exponents of the style.

The Boscawens had owned the Tregothnan estate for five centuries and the early-nineteenth-century phase was the sweeping reconstruction, extension and refacing of their older house on the site rather than a complete new build. The Boscawens rose to prominence in the early eighteenth century. Hugh Boscawen was a courtier and Comptroller of the Household to George I. He was created a Viscount in 1720. His younger brother Edward was the famous admiral who distinguished himself in the Seven Years War. Edward's grandson, another Edward Boscawen, succeeded as 4th Viscount Falmouth in 1808 and was responsible for calling in Wilkins to transform his ancestral home. He himself was advanced to the earldom of Falmouth in the Coronation Honours of George IV. It is interesting how many of the peers George IV created rebuilt their family seats, perhaps both events being signs of their social ambition.

William Wilkins was the Cambridge-educated son of an architect and antiquary and, like his father, combined designing with antiquarian scholarship; in the younger William's case, Grecian as well as

Above: The north front. Wilkins' projecting porte-cochère and staircase tower behind are the principal architectural accents. The blank arcaded crenellation of the parapet and decorated finials and chimney-stacks derive from Wilkins' studies of East Anglian Tudor houses. The right-hand tower was added in the same style by Vulliamy for the 2nd Earl of Falmouth.

Right: The garden front. Wilkins' additions included the south-facing drawing rooms with canted bay windows; the old house was retained in the centre and refaced. On the left is Vulliamy's office wing, which both respects Wilkins' Tudor and improves the overall composition.

English. His 'Tudor' design at Tregothnan shows the fruits of study of East Anglian sixteenth-century houses like East Barsham Manor in Norfolk. It is very similar to Wilkins' contemporary design for the Earl of Rosebery at Dalmeny House in Scotland, begun in 1814. Both houses share the same shallow gables, octagonal turrets, East Barsham finials and mullioned and transomed windows. Much of the impact of Tregothnan comes from its splendidly Picturesque and romantically landscaped site, and the beautiful golden brown of the local Newham stone. Wilkins exhibited his design for the house at the Royal Academy in 1817. Whereas Dalmeny was compressed in execution, Tregothnan spreads its elevations with almost lax abandon.

The key to Wilkins' design is a large central tower containing the staircase with the new main rooms arranged around, while the elevations are handled with a tentative asymmetry. The entrance front is dominated by a projecting porte-cochère which marks the

---

Above: *The library. The bracketed arch divides Wilkins' original space, beyond, from Vulliamy's extension. The Grecian fitted bookcases have gilt wreaths derived from the Choragic Monument of Thrasyllus.*

Left: *The staircase hall. This lofty space is lit by north and south windows in the tower clerestory. The extravagance of the imperial-plan staircase belies the fact that it only serves bedrooms. The iron balustrade and landing arches are conventionally Gothic.*

division between Wilkins' completely new additions to the east and the refaced old house retained on the west. Wilkins' new wing contained a large ballroom and library, characteristic Regency rooms for entertaining, as well as the entrance vestibule and larger staircase hall rising for three storeys into the clerestory tower and giving access all around to the rooms, including the drawing rooms along the south front.

As so often in Regency houses, the scale of the staircase, and its extravagant imperial-plan form, bear no resemblance to the comparatively small and tightly planned bedrooms to which it leads, and is more an impressive and scenic architectural display for its own sake. The spatial impact is enhanced because the visitor approaches from the entrance lobby under one of the side flights, and the complete effect is only grasped when fully under the tower, flooded with light from north and south windows. The plaster ceiling is in the Tudor style, bristling with the badges of Henry VII, Tudor roses and Beaufort portcullises, in cusped panels. The cast-iron balustrade and side arches, however, are straight Gothic.

The principal rooms are all restrained Classical with ordinary detailing, including fluted doorcases, Grecian egg and dart cornices and, mainly, standard 'Belgravian' marble chimneypieces. The

exception is that in the ballroom which was carved by Richard Westmacott the Elder with splendid flanking figures of War and Fame, but this is older than the house and was originally made for another location.

The library is the most impressive room, with fitted Grecian bookcases adorned with gilt wreaths derived from the Choragic Monument of Thrasyllus and a pedimented overmantel. The room was extended for the 2nd Earl of Falmouth by Lewis Vulliamy in 1845–48. Vulliamy also added new service wings and an additional

tower, but sensitively keeping to Wilkins' style, so it is difficult to tell their external work apart. The extension of the library made it more spatially interesting. The date of the addition is given away by the Victorian bracketing of the dividing arch between the old and new parts of the building.

The Regency work at Tregothnan includes a characteristic series of attractive bedrooms, some with their original decoration including maple-grained woodwork and early-nineteenth-century wallpapers in shades of rose and green. The Chinese Bedroom has wallpaper almost identical in pattern to the Chinese wallpaper given by the Prince Regent to Lady Hertford, which she installed at her house, Temple Newsam, near Leeds. Modern Regency amenities included a fitted bathroom and Colza oil chandeliers. Tregothnan has recently been redecorated and the pictures rehung with the advice of Edward Bulmer, but these black-and-white photographs record its appearance in the early 1950s when Christopher Hussey wrote it up as a 'Tudor Brighton Pavilion'.

Above: The Chinese Bedroom. The guest bedrooms at Tregothnan are characteristic of Regency taste and retain some of their original decoration. The Chinese wallpaper is almost identical to that at Temple Newsam, Yorkshire, given by the Prince Regent to Lady Hertford, and is typical of the Regency taste for chinoiserie.

Left: The Small and Large Drawing Rooms. The new entertaining rooms were added to the south and east and are simply Classical in treatment. The Grecian cornices, fluted doorcases and plain marble chimneypieces are no different from those to be found in Belgravia, or other early-nineteenth-century developments in London.

➤ THE WYATTS' CLASSICAL HOUSES ➤

James Wyatt played an important architectural role in the creation of the Regency Classical style with its rich Graeco-Roman detailing, strong colours, and lavish use of marble and *scagliola*. The stylistic formula first evolved in the 1790s was perpetuated for a generation by his sons, Benjamin Dean and Philip, and his nephews, Jeffry and Lewis. The former's unexecuted project for the Waterloo Palace for the Duke of Wellington was the grandest expression of the genre. It was reflected in Philip Wyatt's design for Wynyard Park, County Durham, for the 3rd Marquess of Londonderry (reconstructed after a fire in the 1840s), and in Lewis Wyatt's work at Tatton Park, Cheshire, and especially Willey Park in Shropshire.

James Wyatt told George III that when he returned from Italy (in the late 1760s), he had found architectural taste corrupted by the Adams and that he had been obliged to comply with it. There had been no 'regular' architecture since Sir William Chambers. This is often interpreted as being an opportunistic and cynical remark by

Wyatt, designed to appeal to the King's known preference for Chambers. There is no reason, however, to think that this comment did not reveal Wyatt's true feelings. Although in the 1770s he had perfected a neater, crisper, more economical and elegant version of the Adam manner, at Heveningham and Heaton and his Irish houses, *circa* 1790, his Classical architecture underwent a dramatic change.

In place of the fans, filigree and 'snippets of embroidery' of his early work, there emerged a much more serious, academic, austere

DODINGTON, GLOUCESTERSHIRE Above: *The huge Corinthian porte-cochère covers most of the entrance front and is the major architectural feature of James Wyatt's design. The proportions, with the columns on low stylobates and the shallow pediment, are Grecian, but the Order is Roman Corinthian.*

Right: *The staircase. This huge top-lit extravaganza leads only to suites of small bedrooms. The form pays homage on an exaggerated scale to Sir William Chambers at Carrington House, Whitehall. The staircase balustrade (1812) incorporates ironwork from Fonthill Splendens, and standard gasoliers by Bramah.*

and grand Classical vocabulary, drawing on the example of Sir
William Chambers and also Wyatt's own youthful studies in Rome,
where he had made measured drawings of the Pantheon and other
imperial buildings. This transformation coincided with Wyatt's
appointment in succession to Chambers as Surveyor General of
The King's Works in 1796. It was perhaps the product of a feeling
that now Sir William Chambers' mantle had fallen upon him,
it was his duty to produce an English imperial, academic, Classical
manner.

There was also a practical reason for this sudden dramatic stylistic
change. It was precipitated by the death in or around the early 1790s
of all the craftsmen who had been responsible for the Adam and early
Wyatt style: Joseph Rose for plasterwork, Biagio Rebecca for painted
decoration, and Domenico Bartoli for *scagliola*. This was the team
originally put together by Robert Adam, and whom the Wyatts (to

DODINGTON, GLOUCESTERSHIRE Above: *The dining room,
photographed in 1924. It was later subdivided but has now been restored.
The scagliola pilasters were supplied by Alcott & Browne in 1810. Much of
the wall decoration was originally marbleised and bronzed to match.*

Top: *The library. The main reception rooms are less monumental but richly
finished. The fitted bookcases by Perry & Co. are of mahogany and ebony
with glazed brass grilles and patent locks by Bramah.*

DODINGTON, GLOUCESTERSHIRE Left: *The drawing room with its magnificent
mahogany and satinwood doors.*

Preceding pages: *The entrance hall. The monumental character of the portico is reflected
in this space, 66 feet long, with granite scagliola composite columns and a floor of
Painswick stone, red stone and black marble, inlaid with brass. The coffering and other
details are all of Roman derivation.*

Adam's fury) had taken on wholesale from Kedleston to execute the Pantheon in Oxford Street – James Wyatt's reputation-making first building – in 1770.

Without them, there was no one around who could still execute filigree and festoons. In their place emerged a completely new team, adept at larger scale, less fussy detailing. These included Francis Bernasconi (1762–1841) for plasterwork, Alcott & Browne for *scagliola*, Bramah for metalwork (and water closets), and Richard Westmacott (Junior) for sculpture. These new Wyatt protégées came to dominate the Regency building trades. Bernasconi, in particular, was a genius, equally adept at Gothic and Classical, and worked for most Regency architects as well as all the Wyatts – Nash at Buckingham Palace, Cundy at Grosvenor House, Porden at Eaton Hall, Hopper at Penrhyn, Smirke at Lowther and Eastnor. He was a Londoner of Italian descent, running – from his headquarters near Bedford Square – an efficient stucco factory which relied on repetitive cast mouldings, with only some details being finished on site by hand.

TATTON PARK, CHESHIRE Above: *The entrance hall. The form of Lewis Wyatt's hall with its segmental coffered vault was inspired by that at Carlton House and has similar screens and columns with gryphons and urns on the beams, derived from Desgodetz. The Ionic columns are porphyry* scagliola. *The flutes of the entablature contain upright arrows from the Egerton arms, a neat heraldic touch.*

Right: *Lewis Wyatt's two drawing rooms on the east side of the house retain their original rich furnishing by Gillow. The (replaced) cherry coloured silk of the hangings and upholstery was originally woven at Macclesfield. The last Lord Egerton of Tatton bequeathed the house with all its contents to the National Trust.*

He was typical of the increasing nineteenth-century industrialisation of hitherto hand crafts.

The Bernasconi, Alcott, Bramah, Westmacott team was first fully deployed by James Wyatt at Dodington, Gloucestershire, a house of stupendous quality, built in stages over twenty-five years, from 1796 onwards for Sir Christopher Bethell Codrington, a baronet of medieval descent, but more recently enriched by Jamaican slave sugar. It was only finally completed seven or eight years after Wyatt's own death in 1813. It was this house which first seriously demonstrated Wyatt's academic Classical ambitions, and had so strong an impact on his sons', nephews' and pupils' early-nineteenth-century domestic work. It combines Grecian proportions (of the pediment, for instance) with richest Roman detail. The exterior is austere and monumental, with all demonstration concentrated in the hexastyle portico on the entrance front, a giant porte-cochère deploying the Roman Corinthian Order.

The interior is notable for the very large quota of space (nearly half the floor area) devoted to the entrance and staircase halls, compared to which the principal rooms – library, drawing, breakfast and dining rooms – seem of moderate extent. The staircase hall (designed 1812), in particular, is full height, top lit and occupies all the centre of the

house, with a dramatic imperial-plan staircase and a scenic arcade supporting the landing. It is Wyatt's homage to Chambers and very obviously derived from Carrington House in Whitehall, but much larger. Whereas the prototype had given access to the main reception rooms, that at Dodington leads only to suites of modest family and guest bedrooms. It is pure architectural scenery, out of all proportion to its actual function. In this it was hugely influential on Regency house planning.

The entrance hall, too, is treated as a Roman atrium, 66 feet long, with granite *scagliola* columns, rich brass-inlaid pavement and octagonal coffering from the Temple of Maxentius, and Piranesi-inspired trophies of arms in Bernasconi's stucco coving. It is Wyatt's post-Adam vision of Rome. Both hall and staircase were warmed (and therefore made practically habitable) by patent cast-iron stoves and

WILLEY PARK, SHROPSHIRE Above: *This magnificent Classical house was built on a virgin site in a richly Picturesque park for the 1st Lord Forester, to the design of Lewis Wyatt. Like Dodington and Tatton, it is dominated by a large Corinthian portico-porte-cochère.*

Right: *The staircase rises in two apsidal flights in an oval, domed hall screened from the central hall by pairs of Corinthian sienna scagliola columns. The sequence of entrance hall, main hall and staircase hall fills the whole central axis of Willey and is one of the most impressive processional spaces in any English country house.*

underfloor hot-air heating. There were also Bramah water closets, and gasoliers; for Dodington had one of the earliest systems of gas lighting (in addition to Colza oil) in any English country house.

The Roman style of Dodington had its most successful exponent in James Wyatt's most talented nephew Lewis, who completed Tatton Park, Cheshire (1807–18), for Wilbraham Egerton (a cousin of the Earl of Bridgewater) in similar vein. He designed a large Corinthian portico and entrance hall (inspired by that at Carlton House) with columns of porphyry *scagliola* and details derived from the French architect Antoine Desgodetz's *Les Edifices Antiques de Rome*. But above all, Lewis Wyatt excelled himself at Willey Park, Shropshire (1812–21), for Cecil Weld-Forester, 1st Lord Forester, another George IV Coronation Honours peerage and a Whig brother-in-law of the Duke of Rutland. The Foresters had held land in Wrekin Forest

since the Plantagenets but their late-Georgian wealth derived from the industrial development of the Shropshire coal field around Ironbridge by the Welds, who were merchants from London.

The old house at Willey was down in the valley, but the new house was built on a virgin site on a hill overlooking an incomparable panorama of richly timbered, hilly parkland, and approached by a Picturesque drive several miles long. The landscaping, possibly by John Webb, as at Tatton and other Wyatt houses, included a large lake at the bottom of the lawn below the house. In this grand and wooded setting, the two architectural set-pieces of the exterior, the giant Corinthian portico-porte-cochère and the domed bow read as splendid landscape ornaments.

The influence of Dodington is equally obvious in the interior, where the whole centre is taken up by an atrium hall 40 feet long and nearly 30 feet high with yellow sienna *scagliola* Corinthian columns, brass railed gallery, and segmental plaster vault. The staircase hall beyond is divided from the central hall by columns and comprises a pair of semi-circular sweeps under coffered semi-domes. On the first floor, a bridge connects the top of the stairs to the galleries around the hall. Altogether, this makes up one of the finest processional spaces in an English house.

WILLEY PARK, SHROPSHIRE *Left: The hall. This grandly proportioned, top-lit central space gives access to all the main rooms. It is 40 feet long and nearly 30 feet high, with a segmental vault and brass-railed galleries.*

Below: The library. The domed bow is reflected in an inner apse and there are fitted bookcases of mahogany and brass. The shallow segmental ceiling has bold anthemion decoration, characteristic of the integration of Athenian motifs in the Wyatt Graeco-Roman manner.

Ickworth may not at first sight seem a Regency house. It is the Roman Neo-Classical *folie de grandeur* of the Earl Bishop of Bristol, designed by Mario Asprucci (architect to Prince Borghese) in 1795. The Earl Bishop, however, died on his travels in 1803, in the outhouse of an Italian peasant (who would not allow an heretic prelate into his cottage), and his original plan was never fulfilled. Only the shell of the rotunda and foundation layout of Asprucci's wings were begun, under the direction of Francis Sandys. The house was completed and the interior fitted up and furnished on entirely different lines by the Earl Bishop's son and heir in the 1820s.

The Earl Bishop intended the central block for living and the flanking wings, linked by quadrant corridors, as galleries for the display of his collections of paintings and sculpture. The latter were confiscated by the French Revolutionary armies in Italy, and so never found their way to Ickworth. In the event, the central domed oval became the 'public house' with rooms for entertaining, and the (enlarged) east wing was built as a self-contained family house. This was an exaggerated form of the usual domestic arrangement in large Regency houses, with grand rooms for seasonal entertaining and smaller rooms for private family occupation. The east wing was built and the interior of the rotunda finished in 1820–29. (The west wing was only built in 1845 to balance the composition and has no historic function, though a Real Tennis court was considered.)

Right: *The Neo-Classical rotunda designed by Mario Asprucci of Rome for the Earl Bishop of Bristol in 1795 was incomplete at the time of the latter's death in 1803. The wings planned on either side, originally intended as art galleries, were hardly above ground. When the 1st Marquess came to complete his father's house in the 1820s, he abandoned the Asprucci scheme and built a large east wing as a private family house.*

Below: *The halls. The Earl Bishop had intended the centre of the house to be filled with a complicated spiral staircase. The 1st Marquess installed instead porphyry* scagliola *columns, supplied by the Coade factory.*

This 1820s work was carried out by Frederick William, 5th Earl of Bristol, who was made a marquess in 1826 on the recommendation of his brother-in-law the Prime Minister, Lord Liverpool. He moved into the newly completed house only in 1829. The 1st Marquess had international connections: his younger son was secretary to the British Legation in Madrid, while his sister Elizabeth, Duchess of Devonshire, had retired to live in Rome after 1815.

He himself spent some time travelling on the Continent in the 1820s and bought much in Paris and Italy, as well as through London dealers like Edward Baldock, benefiting from the rich art market in the aftermath of the Napoleonic Wars to acquire French furniture and Old Masters' paintings. He was able to buy Flaxman's *Fury of Athamas*, originally commissioned in Rome by the Earl Bishop. Portrait busts of his wife and his sister were carved by the Florentine sculptor, Lorenzo Bartolini, and in Naples he acquired a large collection of watercolours by François Louis Cassas, the French Neo-Classical landscape artist.

The rotunda and family wing at Ickworth (as well as the town house in St James's Square and a house in Brighton) were furnished *in toto*, including curtains, carpets and fire irons, by Banting, France & Co. (formerly France & Banting), the economical London cabinet-makers who also worked for George IV, furnishing the 'second eleven' guest bedrooms at Windsor Castle.

The principal rooms at Ickworth still retain complete sets of Banting's Regency furniture carried out in fashionable materials: mahogany, rosewood and zebra wood. The bills for the east-wing furniture came to £2,406 in 1827 and £3,100.18.11d in 1829 and included beds, writing tables, dressing tables, games tables, dining tables, bronzed Regency lamps, chimney glasses and large sets of chairs. Banting's bill for the rotunda, including the fitted bookshelves in the library, came to £2,076.13.9d, totalling £7,582 for the house as a whole. Banting also hung the paintings, including the family portraits, which had been stored in their London warehouse while the building work was in progress. The interior fitting-up of Ickworth, therefore, because of the eccentric evolution of the house, was to an exceptional extent the work of a professional furnishing and deco-rating firm.

The actual constructional work was carried out under the 1st Marquess's personal direction by good master craftsmen, including the Bury mason family of De Carle, the carpenter John Trevithen, and the London builder John Field, whose job was 'to complete' all the unfinished work, which he may have designed as well. The *scagliola* columns for the library and entrance hall came from the Coade factory in Lambeth in 1822. The large rooms were treated simply with plain coved ceilings and deep, dentilled Grecian cornices.

The library. This is the largest of the principal rooms, as so often in Regency interiors. It fills the southern part of the rotunda. The sienna scagliola columns were ordered from the Coade factory in 1821 and cost £332. The principal furniture, including the 'extra thick Wilton carpet in crimson and colours', was supplied by Banting, France & Co. The Doric chimneypiece, fixed in 1829, was commissioned by the Earl Bishop in Rome with versions of Canova's Eros & Psyche *and* Bacchus & Ariadne.

Chimneypieces commissioned in Rome by the Earl Bishop, including that in the library by Antonio Canova and his studio, were retrieved from storage and installed in the principal rooms. No architect is mentioned in the accounts, so the adaptation of Asprucci's original design, the new wings, the interior decoration, all seem to have been executed under Lord Bristol's personal direction, using John Trevithen and John Field, the London builders as executants and designer and Bantings, the London furnishers, as the decorators.

Though the house is large and the building project of the 1st Marquess ambitious in scale (900,000 bricks were paid for in 1827), it was by Regency noble standards a relatively economical job and was paid for out of estate income and agricultural profits, as the Herveys, unusually, had no urban or industrial revenues.

Above: *The garden front and west wing.*

Left: *The drawing room. The proportions are the same as the dining room on the other side of the hall. The chimneypiece inlaid with coloured antique marbles was another of those acquired by the Earl Bishop in Rome. The cornice, wall panels and pedimented mahogany doors are all the 1st Marquess's work, executed by John Field. Banting, France & Co. supplied the Wilton carpet, pelmets and some of the furniture, and also hung the magnificent eighteenth-century family portraits by Gainsborough, Reynolds and Angelica Kauffmann. The French eighteenth-century furniture was acquired by the 1st Marquess either in Paris, or through Baldock, the London dealer, for his new rooms at Ickworth.*

❧ OAKLY PARK, SHROPSHIRE ❧

Though only the remodelling of an earlier Georgian red-brick house, Oakly is one of the more architecturally distinguished of Regency houses. It is the work of the admirable C. R. Cockerell for the Hon. Robert Clive (second son of the Earl of Powis and grandson of Clive of India, after whom he was named) and his wife, Baroness Windsor in her own right and co-heiress of Cardiff.

Cockerell was, apart from Soane, the most brilliant synthesist of archaeological scholarship and architectural composition among early-nineteenth-century architects, as demonstrated in his branch offices for the Bank of England or the Ashmolean Museum, Oxford. Oakly, one of his rare country houses, demonstrates the same flair. Cockerell was a pupil of Smirke but his international importance as a Neo-Classicist owed more to his first-hand study of Greek sites, under-

taken from 1810 to 1817 with a group of German scholars, which discovered the Aegina Marbles and the Phygalean Marbles (the latter now in the British Museum).

Robert Clive inherited the Oakly estate from his grandmother in 1817; himself a man of scholarly and artistic tastes, he commissioned Cockerell, a fellow member of the Travellers Club, newly returned from his expedition and relatively unknown as an architect, to replan and remodel the house. Cockerell kept many of the old walls but transformed the place, extending the west range at ground level to make the dining room, study and a circular entrance hall. He incorporated the old dining room to the south as the drawing room and added a new library and breakfast room beyond to the east, leading to a greenhouse or conservatory at the back. A new central staircase hall

was formed on the site of the original small seventeenth-century house, around which the later additions were wrapped. Thus in a remarkably deft way, Cockerell created a perfect Regency plan with grand reception rooms opening up into each other with central doors along an L-shaped axis.

Just as remarkable is the fastidious and scholarly detail of Cockerell's architecture. His new entrance front is a completely original design with two 'porches' composed of the recherché Delian Doric Order *in antis*. That on the right is the entrance; that to the left is for symmetry's sake. The other fronts are simpler with long sash windows and warm red brickwork creating a happily domestic feel, rare in Greek Revival houses. The conservatory was equally original, all of glass with an iron frame, curved roof and urn-capped stone piers. Cockerell's drawings for it are dated 1824. (It was, sadly, dismantled in the mid-twentieth century.)

Above: *Cockerell's south front. The left part incorporates the eighteenth-century drawing room; on the right is the library addition.*

Right: *The entrance hall is given interest by its circular shape and unusual, flat-ribbed, shallow-domed ceiling. Cockerell's design for it is dated 1823.*

Left: *The new west entrance front. Cockerell projected forward the ground floor and created the twin porches with Delian Doric columns. The old house behind is supported on iron girders – Regency engineering underpinning Regency antiquarian scholarship.*

Cockerell's southern porch leads into the circular entrance hall, which has a shallow saucer dome, ornamented with intersecting, flat segmental ribs, a highly unusual design; the cornice is of the simplest Doric form. The wide, paired mahogany doors are ingeniously designed to disguise the fact that the doors are not truly aligned, due to the retention of old fabric.

The *clou* of the house is the full-height staircase hall beyond. The cantilevered stone stairs sweep up around an apse facing the hall door, and the upstairs landing is supported on polished stone columns with the striking, primitive Ionic capitals discovered by Cockerell at the Temple of Apollo at Bassae. Opposite, the upper rear wall is pierced by a fluted colonnade with simplified Corinthian capitals (from the Temple of the Winds at Athens). The frieze above is a part

of Cockerell's set of plaster casts of the Phygalean Marbles. The rest of the set are on the staircase of the Ashmolean Museum, Oxford. Cockerell, as one of the protagonists of the expedition which discovered them, received two sets of these casts. The other (complete) set he gave to his London club, the Travellers, where it today adorns the library designed by Charles Barry.

In the main reception rooms, Cockerell's touch is light but equally scholarly, with simple Grecian friezes and chimneypieces of a strongly personal and archaic character. The library is the finest room. It is a beautifully proportioned space redolent of patrician scholarship. As Christopher Hussey, who was a cousin of the house (and probably inherited his own scholarly gene from his Clive great-grandmother), wrote of this room: 'The Hellenic style was particularly well-suited to libraries because bookcases could be effectively integrated with its rectangular forms. In this pleasing instance, the centre of each wall is regarded as a solid, containing the fireplace, a double door, a wide window, or (in the west side) as separating the windows; and the bookcases as the "curtains" between them, flush on the long wall but projecting a little in the recesses in the end walls. These subtle variations of the rectangular design underline the room's pleasurable effect.'

Left: The staircase hall. This is the architectural climax. Above the landing colonnade can be seen one of Cockerell's plaster casts of the Phygalean Marbles. The ground-floor columns have primitive Ionic capitals from the Temple of Apollo at Bassae, much favoured by Cockerell, and are of polished British 'marble'.

Below: The library. The simple treatment comprises recessed mahogany bookcases and restrained Grecian frieze. The chimneypiece is a typically personal and original Cockerell design with archaic octagonal shafts against a vivid green 'marble' base, thought to be an Irish serpentine. The use of unusual polished stones from the British Isles is redolent of the burgeoning nineteenth-century interest in geology.

III THE GENTLEMAN'S HOUSE

THE Regency saw the heyday of the country gentry. They were rich and free, able to give full reign to personal eccentricity or sporting prowess; while a sound Classical education and travel enabled many of them to become notable architectural patrons and connoisseurs of botany, sculpture and art. As well as improving their estates, they were busy in public life as MPs, JPs, High Sheriffs or officers in the local militia, but they were not yet overburdened with too serious a Victorian sense of Christian responsibility and respectable conformity. They built, gardened, decorated and collected with zest and style. Their houses still represent the wide range of their architectural enthusiasms and cultivated taste, and are among the most attractively habitable of English houses: Southill, Luscombe and Sezincote come high on most lists of desirable houses.

Many of the prominent county families of Victorian, and later, England emerged in this period. The beneficiaries of the first phase of the Industrial Revolution invested their new riches in land, built country houses and set themselves up as landed gentry. Brewers, bankers, mill owners and East India merchants augmented the remaining 'Visitation families' (descendants of the armigerous land-owners recorded by the Tudor and Stuart heralds) and swelled the ranks of the squirearchy in the late eighteenth and early nineteenth centuries.

On the whole, while the longer established families merely modernised and extended their existing houses – and far more houses were altered than built anew – many of the recent squires embarked on the creation of new seats, using both London and good local architects. There were, however, notable exceptions to this rule, and some of the oldest families undertook radical new architectural projects, like Sir Charles Monck (Middleton) at Belsay, who built an austerely scholarly Grecian house in place of the older Border tower-house of his ancestors. On the other hand, Thomas Lister Parker of Browsholme in the Forest of Bowland, who kept the medieval Jacobean house of his family and merely added a new drawing room and dining room designed by Wyatville in a harmonious manner in 1806, may have been more typical of the 'old' families of the time.

The 'new houses' of the period were, as Pevsner has noted, 'a telling illustration of the rarely admitted cultural possibilities of the Industrial Revolution'. Arkwrights, Strutts, Peels, Boultons, Wedgwoods, Watts, Gillows, Barings, Hoares, Whitbreads, and all the rest were impressive architectural patrons and collectors in the early nineteenth century, as they transmogrified into the squirearchy.

SOUTHILL, BEDFORDSHIRE Above: *Marble bust of Henry Holland by George Garrard, commissioned by Samuel Whitbread as a memorial after Holland's death in 1806. Whitbread was responsible for the engraved tribute: 'Thy loss I feel whene'er I see/The labours of thy polished mind ...'*

SEZINCOTE, GLOUCESTERSHIRE Left: *The house showing the onion dome, square panelled Indian chimneys, chajjahs and chattris. Much of the Mogul character comes from this exotic topping. Down below are conventional Georgian windows.*

Preceding pages: *The curving greenhouse and octagonal pavilion.*

❧ SOUTHILL, BEDFORDSHIRE ❧

The estate was bought from the Byngs by the London brewer Samuel
Whitbread I in 1795. His family had come from Cardington in
Bedfordshire originally, and once he had made his fortune in London,
he returned and established himself in his county of origin. A great
many of the entrepreneurs of Georgian England – brewers, iron-
masters, potters, textile manufacturers – came from the yeoman class
or were landless younger sons of lesser gentry. It was natural for
them, when crowned with success, to acquire their own landed estates
in turn and become country squires themselves.

The first Samuel Whitbread died within a year of acquiring Southill
and it was his son, Samuel II, who reconstructed the house. The
Eton-educated younger Samuel was a radical Whig and close friend of
Fox and Sheridan. He chose his architect, Henry Holland, '*architecte
attitré* of the Whig magnates', fresh from his triumph at Carlton
House and nearby Woburn Abbey. Holland's final plans for Southill
are dated 1800. The reconstruction of the house took over ten years
and the fitting and decorating of the interior was not completed until
after 1806, the year of Holland's death. The complete accounts for
the work continue until 1813. Whitbread erected a marble bust by
George Garrard to his architect's memory in the front hall. The
interior has remained unaltered ever since, with all its original
contents, and is the key monument to the first and most elegant phase
of Regency architecture, especially so as Carlton House itself has gone
and its fittings and furnishings absorbed into the more full-blown
splendours of Buckingham Palace and Windsor.

The shell and overall dimensions of the old house at Southill were
retained but totally replanned and remodelled. The exterior, as refaced in Tottenhoe and Portland stone with undemonstrative Ionic
arcades, is extremely reticent, but the interiors are a patrician

Above: *Painting of the reconstruction by George Garrard. This artist was a
protégé of Samuel Whitbread II and also modelled the plaster overdoors of
the entrance hall with horses, bulls, camels, lions and deer.*

Right: *The exterior. Holland merely refaced in stone the existing brick
house. Pevsner described the result as 'the most exquisite English
understatement'.*

Above: *Detail of the drawing room, with restored panels of green and red silk
and elaborate, draped curtains.*

Left: *Detail of painted decoration by André Delabrière, one of the decorators
who had also worked for Henry Holland at Carlton House.*

synthesis of scholarly late-Georgian Graeco-Roman Neo-Classicism expressed with Holland's characteristic restraint and Louis XVI accent. Southill is distinguished by the austerity, precision, elegance and practicality of its interior layout and decoration. It is all 'modern', erudite, rich and refined, and reflects Samuel Whitbread II's almost Roman Republican tastes.

Christopher Hussey in 1930 wrote: 'It is a complete work of art to an extent that is true of few other English houses of any period. Its furniture, its pictures and its ornaments are of the first order, and survive undiminished since the building of the house ... Above all, its exquisite internal decoration ... is of a quality that makes almost every other house a little overdone or a little barbaric in contrast. For Southill must be acknowledged the classic example of the most civilised decade in the whole range of English domestic architecture.'

Like many houses of the date, it is functionally arranged for comfortable living, and conveniently divided into private family rooms in the east wing, and larger 'social' rooms for entertaining in the main block. The former comprise the nursery, a sitting room for Mr

Whitbread, and a boudoir and dressing room for Mrs Whitbread, and were the first interiors to be finished. They display strong Francophile taste with painted decoration by Louis André Delabrière, low-proportioned Gallic chimneypieces and paned and bordered wall hangings of 'rich chintz calico'. The Revd Samuel Johnes, rector of Welwyn, described these rooms in 1800 as 'both beautifully furnished and the latter [the boudoir] the most magnificent, though not at all tawdry, than anything I ever saw ... It looks like a small temple where has been deposited all the rich offerings of every country'.

The drawing room and dining room were completed after 1800. The former shows the influence of Thomas Hope's *Household*

Above: *The dining room. The bow window was added by Holland to create a characteristic Regency room shape. The elegant decoration has been restored recently. The Grecian mahogany furniture was commissioned for the room. The decoration marks the transition towards the full-blown Regency style.*

Opposite right: *The drawing room. The epitome of full-blown Regency taste, fitted up c. 1807. The sumptuous colour scheme with crimson silk on the walls, and the apple green velvet of the upholstery, was restored to the original patterns and tones in the 1990s.*

The entrance hall as remodelled by Henry Holland, with overdoor bronzed plaques of animals by Garrard.

Furniture and Interior Decoration, published in 1807, with its elaborate draped curtains held up by gilt carved eagles, large looking glasses, Grecian sofas, glass chandelier and Egyptian chimneypiece. The furniture at Southill was part designed by Holland and supplied by Regency trade leaders: Morell, Marsh, Lichfield and Thomas Tatham. The textiles were English: Lancashire calico and Manchester velvet. The drawing room and sitting rooms were hung with silk or cotton. The dining room is painted pale green according to Georgian practical convention, with painted 'porphyry' pilaster strips with scrolling vines and Grecian mahogany furniture with lion monopodia.

The interior of Southill was restored in the 1990s and the wall hangings and curtains reinstated to the original design and colouring, with advice from Gervase Jackson-Stops and Edward Bulmer. The colour photographs shown here were taken to illustrate an article recording the restoration work published in April 1994. The black-and-whites were taken for Christopher Hussey's original 1930 articles, which formed part of *Country Life*'s influential championing of the Regency style between the Wars.

LUSCOMBE CASTLE, DEVON

Charles Hoare, a younger son of the Hoares of Stourhead and partner in the family bank, bought an estate on the Devon coast near Dawlish because the climate suited the delicate health of his wife, Dorothea Robinson. They called in Humphry Repton and John Nash, then in brief partnership, to build a new house there and to landscape the park. Mrs Hoare, with Repton's help, chose the site for the new house in a secluded valley, 'sheltered by its own hills, with no intrusive alien property, and the best possible Aspect to the Sea, which rises over a village of which the unsightly parts are hid'. So Repton extolled the place in his Red Book. The southern view down the valley he described as 'an interesting picture which requires only to be framed by an adequate foreground of highly dressed Lawn and Pleasure Garden on which trees or shrubs may be planted to vary the surface'. And so he went to work, creating the archetypal Picturesque landscape, dressing the foreground and framing the valley with wooded belts.

He recommended that the new house be given the 'Character of a Castle', rather than a Grecian villa, to complement the setting, 'with bold irregularity of outline'. His 'ingenious friend, Mr Nash'

Above: *The library. The largest of the rooms, it was originally the dining room. The Nash bookcases with brass-latticed grills were moved here later.*

Left: *The entrance, forming a Gothic porte-cochère.*

Below: *The exterior seen from the south. The house nestles into the secluded setting, landscaped by Repton.*

produced a design that combined 'internal arrangement and convenience' with an external outline 'which must always please the Eye of Taste'. Nash's design is one of the prettiest and most compact of his castle houses, the major accent being a central octagonal tower, and the elevations handled with considered irregularity and enlivened with bays and windows of varied tracery.

The skyline is diversified with battlements and groups of shafted chimney-stacks. All the ground-floor windows are full length, according to Regency fashion, whereby the landscape and the house flow into each other, and a Gothick conservatory was incorporated in the design, heated in winter by a hot-air flue.

The Gothic lines of the exterior, as usual, extended inwards no further than the circulation spaces, and all the main rooms were Classical, detailed by Nash in a modest and economical Grecian idiom. They were furnished by Thomas Chippendale the Younger, and the chairs and tables of mahogany and satinwood are very similar to those provided for Charles Hoare's elder half brother, Sir Richard Colt Hoare, at Stourhead at the same time.

Above (left): The drawing room designed by Nash, with arched inset bookcases, and the ceiling painted to resemble a sky. The furniture was supplied by Chippendale the Younger c. 1803; (right): The alcove off the drawing room.

Left: The circular vestibule. This geometrical space is the crux of the internal layout and gives access to all principal areas: the entrance hall to the north, drawing room to the south, (original) eating room to the east, staircase hall and (original) library to the west. The furniture at Luscombe, including the sleek Grecian hall chairs shown here, was supplied by Thomas Chippendale the Younger.

The house was begun in 1799, and the interior was fitted up and furnished in 1802–03, work being completed by 1804. The building of Luscombe is remarkably fully documented. As well as Repton's Red Book, all Nash's annotated drawings survive, as do detailed building accounts for the whole project. As usual, in a Nash–Repton house, the library was the principal living room and there were also bookcases in the octagonal drawing room.

In the mid-nineteenth century, the rooms were reorganised: a billiard room was added and the original dining room converted to the library, to which the bookcases were moved. Subsequently, a large new church designed by Gilbert Scott was built adjoining the end of the west service wing. On the whole, however, these Victorian alterations were sympathetic, and Luscombe survives as a triumph of the Picturesque in both its architecture and landscaping. As Christopher Hussey noted, it is more or less contemporary with, and puts into practice to a notable degree, the principles adumbrated in Uvedale Price's *Essays on the Picturesque* (1794), Payne Knight's *The Landscape* (1794), and Humphry Repton's own *Sketches and Hints on Landscape Gardening* (1795).

Luscombe is a house which was consciously composed together with its landscape setting to form a single Picturesque work of art. It survives with its original contents and oak- and cedar-dotted park as a remarkable Regency ensemble. The Hoares of Luscombe, who in the twentieth century inherited the family baronetcy from their Stourhead cousins, still own and live in the house.

≫ SHERINGHAM, NORFOLK ≪

Sheringham Hall on the Norfolk coast was Repton's 'most favourite work'. It was created for Abbot and Charlotte Upcher in 1812–17. By then, Repton's alliance with Nash had come to an end and he was assisted in the architectural details by his son, John Adey Repton. Like Luscombe, Sheringham was an unostentatious, comfortable, compact house for a young married couple in their twenties, and was not intended for grand entertaining. Much of the effort went into siting the house, shelter planting and landscaping the park, as demonstrated by Repton's Red Book. It was Repton's ideal, as he makes clear in the reference in *Fragments on the Theory and Practice of Landscape Gardening* (1816).

The site was a new one for a country house (the proximity to the seaside was an aspect of Regency taste); only a 'farmhouse' existed on the property when the Upchers bought the estate for £52,000 in 1811. 'They found paradise, and there they began their "bower",' as the Upchers' daughter recorded. Unlike Luscombe, where Repton had adumbrated the Picturesque outlines of Nash's castellated house as the perfect foil to the landscape, at Sheringham the house was a plain, 'modern', Classical design of cream brick, with bow windows and novel casements employing large panes of plate glass. The only exposed Classical details of the exterior, apart from the proportions, are the south colonnade and Roman Doric entrance porch. Away from Nash's influence, this simple, well-proportioned, comfortable architecture was Repton's preferred mode.

The Upchers themselves, with a young family and a quiet, domestic way of life, had strong views on the way the house was to be planned

Above: *Repton's Red Book, 1812. As architect for the new house, Repton employed his son, John Adey. The original design was larger than the executed scheme, in which the centre was contracted from five to three bays. The Upchers did not want a large house but a cosy 'bower' just for themselves and their growing family.*

Right: *The south front is sheltered from the North Sea by the wooded hill behind. Immediately after acquiring the property, in June 1812, Abbot Upcher noted 'Repton met us at Sheringham' and helped to select the exact site for the new house. The unusual bow windows were a design of Repton's own, with large panes to catch the views.*

Above: *John Adey Repton's design for the staircase shows the original intention, with coloured glass in the tall, arched window. It represented Repton's ideal of 'elegance without extravagance'.*

Right: *The corridor. The plan of Sheringham was practical and straightforward. A square entrance hall led to a cross-corridor off which opened the eating room to the south, the library-living room to the east, and the staircase to the north. A small 'parlour' for Mrs Upcher and a 'Justice Room' for Mr Upcher completed the accommodation. These 1957 photographs show the Gillow furniture collected by Thomas Upcher in the mid-twentieth century and since sold.*

and used. They wanted 'no useless drawing room', just a library-living room and eating room, and a business room for him and sitting room for her. This chimed with Repton's own views, for he was a strong proponent of 'one large living room to contain ... everything requisite to modern comfort ...'.

Sadly, Abbot Upcher died in 1819, and the interior was not fully fitted up until the 1830s, when his son, Henry, moved in and lived there for fifty-three years. Nevertheless, the 'living room' at Sheringham with its rosewood shelves, palmette cornice, Carrara marble chimneypiece and comfortable (albeit early Victorian) seat furniture is a good demonstration of Repton's intention.

In the 1950s, when Christopher Hussey wrote up the house in *Country Life*, Sheringham belonged to Abbot Upcher's descendant Thomas. He was one of the mid-twentieth-century Regency Revival pioneer collectors and decorated and furnished the house accordingly. After his death, his collection of Gillow pieces was sold, but the house and park were acquired by the National Trust and the library retains its old decoration and furnishings.

Above: The staircase. The stone cantilevered staircase rises in an apse and has the simplest of bannister rails. The statues in the niches were commissioned in the 1950s (following a Repton idea) from an American sculptor, Barbara Roett.

Right: The living room. The palmated frieze and marble chimneypiece were designed by J. A. Repton. The room represents the Repton ideal of a comfortable, informal library for everyday use. Sheringham was designed with no other drawing room. The rosewood bookcases and seat furniture were only supplied in 1839, for Abbot Upcher's son, Henry, completing Repton's original concept. (The wallpaper and carpet are later Victorian.)

SEZINCOTE, GLOUCESTERSHIRE Above: *The Coade stone fountain
in front of the conservatory.*

Right: *The conservatory. This sweeping quadrant terminating in an octagonal pavilion
acts as a Picturesque counter-balance to the main block.
It was always faced in a greyer stone, marking its subsidiary character.*

≫ SEZINCOTE, GLOUCESTERSHIRE ≪

> And there they burst on us, the onion domes,
> Chajjahs and chattris made of amber stone,
> "Home of the Oaks", exotic Sezincote!
> Stately and strange it stood, the Nabob's house,
> Indian without and coolest Greek within.
> *(From 'Summoned by Bells', John Betjeman)*

Colonel John Cockerell bought the estate in 1795 on his return from Bengal, but died soon after, leaving only illegitimate children. He was succeeded by his third brother, Charles, who employed another brother, the architect Samuel Pepys Cockerell, to design a new house for him in Mogul style. Charles Cockerell (created a baronet in 1809) had also served in the East India Company, and Samuel Pepys Cockerell was Surveyor to the East India Company. The new house celebrated these Indian connections, with the help of Thomas and William Daniell, the artists. Thomas had spent ten years in India painting and drawing the architecture and scenery, and knew more about Indian architecture than any living European.

Humphry Repton was also involved in the design of Sezincote. Though no Red Book survives, he refers to his role at Sezincote in his *Designs for the Pavilion at Brighton*: 'I had been consulted [*circa* 1805] by the owner of Sezincote where he wished to introduce the gardening and architecture which he had seen in India ... I gave my opinion, even assisted in selecting forms from Mr T. Daniell's collection of drawings. Yet the architectural department, of course, devolved to the brother of the proprietor.' Repton added that in S. P. Cockerell's designs 'the detail of Hindu architecture is as beautiful as it appears

Above: The staircase. The interiors are conventionally Neo-Classical. The staircase leads to the principal rooms on the piano nobile. It is an unusual design beginning with two flights converging in one, supported on structural cast-iron girders.

Left: The saloon. The bow window, the form of the curtains, the trompe l'œil gilt trellised cove, and the large looking glasses all survive from the original 1820s decoration, and make this a pure Regency interior.

in the drawings, and comparable with pure Gothic's richness of effect.' Despite Repton's involvement and possible supervision of the general landscape, it seems to have been Thomas Daniell who advised specifically on the layout of the Water Garden, or Thornery, and the treatment of various 'Hindu' structures there, including a shrine with a Coade figure of Sourya, the sun god, and a bridge inspired by the Elephant Caves near Bombay.

The new Sezincote was built on the site of the old manor house (shown on an estate map of 1704). The main block is a disguised Classical rectangle, but fitted to the site according to Picturesque principles by an asymmetrical curving greenhouse terminating in an octagonal pavilion. Much of the exotic architectural impact comes from the skyline with 'Indian' chimneys, 'chajjahs and chattris' (overhanging cornices and lantern-like corner pavilions), and the dominant central onion dome. The main block is faced in beautiful golden Barrington stone and the greenhouse quadrant wing in a greyer stone, emphasising its architectural role as a counterpoint. Both stones were skilfully carved with frilly Mogul ornament by local Cotswold masons.

The principal block is low and spreading and contains the 'social' rooms on a *piano nobile* over a 'basement' storey with an everyday dining room and smaller family room, but there is no bedroom floor. The bedrooms and offices were all fitted into subsidiary wings behind. The interior, as so often in Regency houses, regardless of external style, is thoroughly Classical. The entertaining rooms on the *piano nobile* are approached by a magnificent flying staircase supported on cast-iron girders, top-lit from large 'fanlight' windows above. The balustrade is cast in bronze with sparing use of Greek anthemion ornament. The interior decoration continued into the 1820s and work was still going on in 1827 when C. R. Cockerell (S. P.'s son) added the office wing at the back.

The saloon fills the bow in the centre of the south front and has a high coved ceiling. The large looking glasses, gilt and painted *trompe l'œil* lattice pattern on the cove, and the (restored) original arrangement of draped curtains hanging from a carved gilt eagle and gilded lion masks are splendid examples of Regency interior decoration. Sir Charles's own bedroom was a military tent room with draperies hung from spears, but that had to be dismantled after falling into a derelict state in the 1940s. The house and gardens have been well restored and enhanced by the present owners, Mr and Mrs Peake, and Mrs Peake's father, the banker Sir Cyril Kleinwort, who bought the estate after the Second World War.

The bridge was designed by Thomas Daniell, who was responsible for the Water Garden, or Thornery, and the architectural features around it. The bridge was inspired by the Elephant Caves near Bombay. The sejant bulls on the parapet were originally Coade stone, but have been replaced in cast iron.

⇒ BELSAY HALL, NORTHUMBERLAND ⇐

The Belsay estate had belonged to the Middletons since the thirteenth century. Their medieval tower house still survives. Sir William Middleton (1738–95), 5th Baronet, created the present landscape park. His son Charles (1779–1867), who took the name Monck as a result of an inheritance from his maternal grandfather (additional estates in Lincolnshire), extended his father's park, moved the village and built a new house to his own design. Belsay Hall is among the most thorough-going examples of Greek Revival architecture in England, and a demonstration of the impact of a Classical education and foreign travel on the visual taste of a Northumbrian squire.

Sir Charles and his wife had undertaken an extensive tour on their honeymoon, from September 1804 to April 1806. Because of the Napoleonic Wars, they were forced to avoid large areas of standard Grand Tour Europe, and instead visited Germany, Austria and Asia Minor, taking in Prague, Vienna, Trieste, Venice and Athens. He made a personal study of the Acropolis monuments and was greatly influenced by ancient Greek architecture. In Athens, he was joined

by Sir William Gell, another Hellenist baronet who helped him in the evolution of the scheme for Belsay.

On his return, he designed his 'new mansion' over the winter of 1806–07. More than three hundred drawings for it survive, in his own hand. It replaced the old family seat at Belsay Castle, where the fifteenth-century tower and 1614 range were retained as ornaments in the grounds, though the modern (i.e. eighteenth-century) wings were demolished. The stone for the new house was quarried on the site of the old village (replaced with a model layout of arcaded cottages, also designed by Sir Charles, on the edge of the park). The foundations of the new house were laid in summer 1807. Construction took ten years, and Sir Charles and his family moved in during 1817, the

---

Above: The entrance front. The proportions and detail of Belsay, as designed by its owner Sir Charles Monck (Middleton) in 1807, were derived from the Theseion in Athens and other Greek sources studied on his honeymoon.

Right: The Doric portico in antis. The fluted columns are made from blocks without mortar and the precise sizes of the ashlar masonry, which was quarried in the garden, were worked out by Sir Charles to three decimal places.

bedrooms and entrance side then being complete, but fitting up the other main rooms took longer, and the outbuildings were not finished until the 1830s.

Sir Charles was single-minded in a way that a professional architect might not have been. He successfully married the requirements of a Regency house – library, drawing room, dining room, comfortable bedrooms and impressive hall – to the resemblance of an Ancient Greek temple. His particular source was the Theseion in Athens. The proportions and detail, including the fluted Doric columns in the entrance at Belsay, are all identical with the Theseion, and the outline plan of the house is a square of 100 feet, as is that of the Theseion.

Left: *The central hall. This splendid peristyle interior is executed entirely in the local cream-coloured sandstone. Each of the Ionic capitals was carved by a different mason. It is like the cella of a Grecian temple. A richer note is supplied by the scrolling brass balustrade, designed by Sir Charles's sister on the model of Cundy's Northumberland House staircase in London.*

Below: *The library. This was the largest of the principal rooms, well proportioned and full of light from four tall sash windows. The simple plasterwork includes an anthemion frieze copied from the Erectheion on the Acropolis. The bookcases, too, are derived from the Erectheion. The original Regency furniture shown in the photograph has been sold, and the interior of Belsay is now preserved as an empty monument by English Heritage.*

Belsay makes an instructive companion with Oakly where C. R. Cockerell, who had also studied Greek buildings at first hand, successfully integrated scholarly Greek details and Orders into ordinary English, domestic, red-brick architecture. Belsay is more uncompromising and shows a much stricter archaeological approach. Sir Charles was also a mathematician and he put a large effort into the proportions of his house, working out the precise sizes of individual blocks of stone, and the joints between them, to three decimal places. This attention is responsible for the almost monolithic-seeming quality of the fine sandstone ashlar masonry of the exterior walls. It completes an architectural effect which is, in Hussey's phrase, a 'scholar's idealising recreation of Ancient Greece'.

Belsay is a splendidly scaled house. The entrance on the east front is marked by a pair of full-height Doric columns *in antis*. The other elevations are completely plain; the windows cut in without architraves, and only a massive triglyph frieze all around. Take away the windows and it *is* a Greek temple. The core of the house is a full-height, top-lit central hall, or peristyle, with two tiers of fluted columns. Those on the ground floor have Ionic capitals, each carved by a different mason and put in place in 1812. John Dobson of Newcastle, the local architect (*see pages 168–70*), helped Sir Charles

with the full-scale drawings for these capitals. He later said that Sir Charles had 'much raised the standard of good mason work in the North of England'. This space, too, gives a remarkably convincing impression of the *cella* of a Greek temple.

Most of the interior of Belsay, however, comprises ordinary and practical Regency rooms, the Greek detail being restricted to plaster cornices, the moulding of door architraves, and the chimneypieces. The main rooms were arranged to face east, south and west – catching the light throughout the day, while the domestic offices were on the north side. An interesting detail is the use of paired sashes with stone mullions on the south front. This is an 'incorrect', Northern, almost vernacular detail aimed at increasing light and one which Sir Charles saw the practical benefit of. He also used local oak for the joinery, not mahogany.

Despite its archaeological exactitude, Sir Charles's new house showed much common sense and must have been comfortable, with well-proportioned, well-lit, unostentatious rooms. The largest is the south-facing library, with detailing inspired by the Erectheion on the Acropolis. It is difficult to judge now, as all the original furniture has been sold and Belsay is preserved as an empty monument in the guardianship of English Heritage, while the family live in another house on the estate.

The full impact of Belsay comes from the landscape setting. The house sits on a massive square, stone reveted and arcaded terrace, with views over the Georgian landscape park. To the north-west is the stable block (completed in 1832), its clock turret based on the Tower of the Winds in Athens. To the east stretches a Romantic garden, making dramatic use of the quarry which produced the stone for the house, and where Sir Charles planned the cuttings to create narrow clefts or ravines with this ultimate effect in mind.

Punctuated with tall arches, and exotically planted, these mysterious walks – like a sacred Greek landscape – link the new house to the old castle, a preserved Romantic tableau, which forms the terminus and final climax of the layout. The drama and lush planting of the Picturesque setting forms the perfect foil and backdrop for the cerebral and austere Neo-Classical architecture of the house, the earliest and most consistent of pure Greek Revival houses.

Belsay in its landscape setting. The severity of the house is offset by the lushness of the park and garden planting. The stables in the distance were only completed in 1832, and the clock turret is inspired by the Tower of the Winds in Athens.

❧ BIGNOR PARK, SUSSEX ❧

Bignor Park near Petworth is an interesting example of the younger
son of a landed family making a fortune, buying an estate of his own
elsewhere and building a new house. John Hawkins came from
Cornwall, but made his own money as a Levant merchant in London.
He bought the Bignor estate, originally one of twelve medieval parks
of the Earls of Arundel, in 1806. He was also a scholar, Fellow of the
Royal Society, excavator of the Roman villa discovered at Bignor in
1811, and had travelled in Greece, like Monck, Gell and Cockerell.
The Classical past and the Italianate views towards the South Downs
were significant factors at Bignor in choosing the site and Classical
style of the new house, which replaced a decayed Elizabethan manor
house. The Sussex historian James Dallaway wrote of Bignor in 1832
that it was 'difficult to point out a spot where the scenery of Sussex
appears to so much advantage'. Hawkins employed as his architect
Henry Harrison, son of a London surveyor, who had a large practice
designing lesser country houses.

The new Bignor was begun in 1826 and completed in 1828 at a
total cost of £10,250. Harrison's design is the epitome of Regency
stripped Classical simplicity, and its square proportions and large
windows seem proto-twentieth century. It was this 'modern'
appearance which appealed to Lord Mersey when he bought the
estate in 1926. He refurnished the interior in Regency style, buying
objects from Edward Knoblock's Beach House, Worthing, including
architectural murals on glass originally painted by Sir William
Nicholson for Knoblock's apartment in the Palais Royal, the
incunabulum of the Regency Revival. It was houses like Bignor that
some twentieth-century architects and critics looked to as a jumping-
off point for a 'modern' English architectural style.

Above: *The south front. Henry Harrison's spare Classical architecture relies
on good proportions and large windows.*

Right: *The library as simplified in the 1920s. The bookcases were originally
pedimented and grained to resemble oak.*

THE HOUSES OF SIR JOHN SOANE

Most of Soane's significant country houses were designed in the 1780s and 1790s when he evolved a distinctive compact villa plan, often with a bowed centre and round-arched windows. His best surviving houses, such as Saxlingham, Shotesham, Letton and Tyringham, are all pre-Regency and of this type. His personal idiosyncratic Neo-Classical manner also emerged in the same period. Though deploying a rich international Roman style for 'palaces' and public buildings, Soane developed simpler, more original, Classical forms for the gentleman's house. This personal language was largely astylar and made extensive use of incised linear mouldings, segmental arches, top lighting, and shallow domes or cross-vaulted ceilings (derived from his old master, George Dance). It made possible innovative spatial effects aimed at dissolving the sense of enclosure in rooms. Soane's houses are also notable for his eccentric use of scholarly Classical details: Greek key, *paterae*, sarcophagi and *acroteria*, representing the 'symbolic language of Antiquity'.

The 'simplicity', linear qualities and spatial originality of Soane's domestic architecture appealed to twentieth-century taste, even if his scholarly architectural vocabulary was misunderstood. His seeming plainness and neurotic oddness earned him few admirers in the later nineteenth century or early twentieth century, however, and many of his houses were radically remodelled, or demolished, before they could be recorded by *Country Life*. It is only in recent years that the architecture of Soane's later houses has been appreciated and restored, at Moggerhanger and Wotton, and subsequently properly photographed by the magazine.

Though the most original genius among Regency architects, Soane was mainly involved after 1800 in public work, so his country houses

PORT ELIOT, CORNWALL Above: *The drawing-room ceiling. The circular drawing room, created by Soane in 1804, has a ceiling decorated with a radiating Greek key pattern. The free and often eccentric use of Greek key ornament was a leitmotif of Soane's personal architectural vocabulary.*

PITZHANGER MANOR, EALING Right: *The entrance front was designed by Sir John Soane, for himself, in November 1800 and built 1801–03. It was inspired by the Arch of Constantine in Rome. The Classical roundels depict the Medici Lion. The architectural scale is surprisingly grand for a small rural villa, and was similar to Soane's contemporary Lothbury Court arch at the Bank of England.*

are scarce. In his last decades, from 1820 onwards, he only squeezed two country house jobs, Wotton and Pell Wall, into a schedule entirely devoted to Westminster offices, law courts, Commissioners' churches and other national buildings. In the first decade of the century, apart from alterations and additions, he was responsible for three significant surviving country house works: Pitzhanger Manor (his own villa at Ealing), the remodelling of Port Eliot, Cornwall, and Moggerhanger in Bedfordshire. All three display aspects of his architectural genius, though none is entirely a straight Soanic design or a complete new-build.

Soane bought Pitzhanger Manor at Ealing for himself in 1800. He had several friends, including John Winter, Solicitor to the Bank of England, in this once pleasant and accessible area, which made it the ideal spot for a country retreat. There he could spend the weekends and entertain his friends. Pitzhanger was sold to Soane by the family of George Gurnell, a City merchant and father-in-law of George Dance, who had extended the house in 1768. Soane bought the property in August 1800 for £4,500.

He immediately began remodelling, keeping Dance's wing, but building a new main block and kitchen offices, as well as outworks like artificial ruins and an entrance archway. One of Soane's aims at Pitzhanger was to interest his sons in architecture, a plan which singularly failed. His disappointment turned the Pitzhanger dream to ashes and he sold the property after only a few years, removing his collections to his museum in Lincoln's Inn Fields. It later became the public library of a London suburb, a gloomy fate, though one which saved it from demolition.

The new main block was a brilliant Neo-Classical exercise. The front elevation was expressed as a Roman triumphal arch, with attached Ionic columns and free-standing Coade-stone figures inspired by the caryatids of the Erectheion. It had parallels with his contemporary archway in the Lothbury Court of the Bank of England. The new block contained a breakfast parlour, with a shallow domed ceiling on segmental arches, and a library with a cross-vaulted ceiling.

The walls of both were enlivened with niches for cinerary urns and sarcophagi – the 'neo-classical furniture of death' (in Summerson's phrase), making both rooms archetypical Soane statements. The dining room and drawing room occupied the retained Dance wing, the latter hung with Chinese wallpaper. Building work was completed and the house ready for occupation in 1804.

Port Eliot in Cornwall was a more conventional country seat of the Eliot family (whose London houses had already been repaired and altered by Soane). In 1804, the year John Eliot succeeded to the family barony, Soane was consulted to reconstruct the then part-medieval and part-eighteenth-century house, and to draw up plans for new south and east fronts with entertainment rooms. The resulting exterior elevations are uninspired rubble-stone 'Gothic'

TYRINGHAM HALL, BUCKINGHAMSHIRE *The entrance front and the Soane bridge.*

with castellated parapets and plain arched windows. They could have been designed by anybody. The new interior, however, which comprised a dining room, library and drawing room – the usual social rooms to be found in a Regency house – is architecturally distinguished. These were treated by Soane in his characteristic Neo-Classical manner with deceptively simple proportions and idiosyncratic detail.

The drawing room is circular and has a ceiling formed of a radiating, geometrical, elongated Greek key pattern, which Soane adopted from Nicholas Revett and made a leitmotif of his personal style. The large rectangular dining room also deploys Soanic Greek key, especially in the chimneypiece of inlaid black-and-white marble. The library was later converted into a drawing room and has lost its bookcases. The house was further remodelled with new entrance and office wings in a more full-blooded medieval vein by Henry Harrison *circa* 1829, but Soane's Neo-Classical rooms survive as little altered examples of the architect's personal manner and were photographed by *Country Life* in 1948.

The most complete Soane Regency house to survive is Moggerhanger in Bedfordshire. This had been bought by Godfrey Thornton, a director of the Bank of England, for whose family Soane had worked elsewhere. Some additions to the unpretentious existing building were made in 1791 but the major extension and remodelling took place for his son, Stephen Thornton, in 1809–11. A new entrance front was created, comprising a three-storeyed centre with pierced balustrade, flanking wings and a semi-circular porch of Greek Doric columns. The windows in the entrance front were round-arched. Those on the ends of the flanking wings were framed in Soanic aedicules, with simplified Grecian pediments and *acroteria*, while the house was faced in Parkers Roman cement to resemble stone. This ensemble synthesized the austere Neo-Classical forms with personal 'antique' detailing peculiar to Soane.

A hospital for most of the twentieth century, Moggerhanger has recently been fully restored by a private trust under the direction of the architect Peter Inskip. As a result, it can now be seen as one of Soane's finest surviving country houses, and was published for the first time in *Country Life* in 2005.

MOGGERHANGER, BEDFORDSHIRE *Recent restoration by a private trust, after long use as a hospital, has revealed this to be one of Soane's finest surviving country houses.*

The staircase and landing (left above and right) *are spatially linked. The iron balustrade is almost identical to the one in Sir John Soane's Museum, London.*

Left: *The garden front. The incised pilasters are characteristic of Soane.*

❧ REGIONAL ARCHITECTS ❧

Flourishing provincial architects had been a strong feature of Georgian England: Carr of York, the Smiths of Warwick, the Bastards of Blandford. This pattern continued in the Regency period with many counties, cities and regions having their own pre-eminent local architectural firm: Dobson of Newcastle, the Websters of Kendal, Lindley of Doncaster, Foster of Liverpool, the Haycocks of Shrewsbury and the Trubshaws of Staffordshire.

In particular, the rapid industrial and urban development of the Midlands and the North created great opportunities and ensured that competent local architects were kept busy with varied buildings for the growing towns, as well as new houses for the landed gentry and villas for the mercantile and professional classes. Typically, the Regency provincial architect was the offspring of a family of builders who had trained as a more sophisticated architect under a leading practitioner either in a regional centre or in London.

Thus, John Foster (Junior) had been entrusted by his father to James and Jeffry Wyatt's offices in London before returning to Liverpool to dominate the architectural profession there. George

Webster of Kendal had been sent by his builder father, Francis, to William Atkinson in Manchester, with whom he had come into contact as the contractor for his house at Clapham Lodge, Ingleton.

JOHN DOBSON OF NEWCASTLE

Probably the most talented of Regency provincial architects, John Dobson had trained both under the local architect, David Stephenson, and in London in the studio of the artist John Varley, where he came into the orbit of Sir Robert Smirke before returning north to dominate the architectural scene in County Durham, Northumberland and north-east Cumberland.

Apart from his well-known work in Newcastle itself, Dobson was pre-eminently a country house architect and he altered or designed over one hundred houses, working especially for 'the beneficiaries of

MELDON PARK, NORTHUMBERLAND Above: *The garden front with its austerely simple architecture and fine ashlar stone.*

Right: *The entrance front with Greek Ionic porch and simple corner pilasters.*

the industrial revolution', whether new rich manufacturers or old landed families enriched by coal royalties. He specialised both in competent Tudor Gothic, as at Beaufront and Lilburn, and simplified, scholarly Classicism.

His Greek Revival buildings were most admired at the time and have secured his posthumous reputation. Well-planned, meticulously detailed and excellently built, they are handsome and habitable. His simplest designs, relying on good ashlar masonry and precise proportions and detailing, are among the more 'modern'-seeming Regency houses, especially admired in the twentieth century. Their plans, too, are characteristically Regency with a library, dining room and drawing room forming the principal social rooms, arranged around over-scaled staircase halls and often an integrated greenhouse as an attractive feature in northern climes: Nunnykirk, Longhirst, Mitford and Meldon are among his finest Grecian houses.

Meldon Park was designed for Isaac Cookson, whose fortune derived from coal, and whose descendants still own it. Completed in 1832, it was one of the latest of Dobson's fine series of Grecian Northumberland houses, and has many similarities with Nunnykirk, designed in 1825. It is large and plain. The garden front is, by coincidence or morphic resonance, almost identical to Henry

Harrison's south front at Bignor Park, Sussex (*see page 160*), which has similar proportions, the same austere tripartite arrangement and the same window pattern, but Meldon is executed in very fine ashlar stone, rather than stucco. The lower north-east wing contains a conservatory similar to the arrangement at Dobson's Longhirst. The interior has heavy Grecian detail in the main rooms. The imperial-plan staircase was altered in 1930 by Lutyens, who changed the bannister design.

THE WEBSTERS OF KENDAL

Francis, the father, and George, the son, covered a similar geographical area to Dobson, but on the other side of the Pennines, including Westmorland, Lancashire and part of the West Riding along the main turnpike from London to Kendal, via Skipton. Like Dobson, the Websters were equally adept at Tudorbethan and Greek Revival. Their houses in the former style, like Underley, Whelprigg and

---

MELDON PARK, NORTHUMBERLAND Right: *The staircase hall. This over-scaled and grandiose central space is typical of Regency planning. (The balustrade was replaced by Lutyens, c. 1930.)*

Below: *The library, with heavy Grecian coved plaster ceiling and fitted bookcases, was, as usual, the principal living room of the house.*

Whittington, were remarkably precocious and included regional features, like stepped mullion and transom windows and even pseudo pele-towers, creating in-built history, as if sixteenth-century houses had been added to medieval fortifications.

Like Dobson, the Websters were noted for the high quality of their masonry, making use of precisely cut ashlar blocks, refined tooling techniques and weather-shot joints. They were descended from a dynasty of stonemasons and had their own marble works in Kendal, where local stones – like Dent marble or Shap granite – were cut and polished, and despatched by canal all over the country to the order of other architects. (The Wyatville-designed chimneypieces of Dent marble in the Guard Room and St George's Hall at Windsor Castle, for instance, were supplied by the Websters.)

In cutting stone and 'marble', they used modern machinery, thus representing at a regional level the industrialisation of Regency building trades. The success of their local 'marbles' was also a reflection of the Regency fashion for British stones and characteristic of early-nineteenth-century taste – slate and Mona marble at Penrhyn, Irish serpentine and Welsh 'porphyry' at Oakly, fossil marble in all the

Webster houses, white Painswick and red Forest of Dean stone in the hall floor at Dodington.

Also like Dobson, George Webster was master of a reticent, scholarly, Classical manner, particularly suited to the austere grandeur of northern landscapes. With their smooth masonry, domed bows and tripartite windows, these houses show the influence, at one remove – through William Atkinson – of the Wyatts: as is demonstrated in houses like Read (cotton) and Rigmaden (banking). The best preserved Atkinson and Webster Classical house is Broughton

BROUGHTON HALL, YORKSHIRE Above: *The White Drawing Room. Originally added by Atkinson, this was remodelled by George Webster for Sir Charles Tempest when he became the first post-Reformation Catholic High Sheriff of the West Riding (following the Emancipation Act in 1829). The paintings were acquired by Stephen and Elizabeth Tempest on their Grand Tour of Italy in 1817. All the furniture here and elsewhere at Broughton was supplied by Gillow of Lancaster.*

Right: *The entrance front. The sixteenth-century seat of the Tempests, an ancient recusant Catholic family, was entirely remodelled in the Regency period. The flanking wings were added in 1809–11 by William Atkinson; the main block was refaced by George Webster, and the porte-cochère and the bedroom wing added with a chapel belfry to make a Picturesque Classical composition in perfect harmony with the landscape, like Chatsworth.*

Hall near the Lancashire–West Riding border. This was not the seat of a 'new' family but an ancient, recusant Catholic dynasty, the Tempests, who could prove an unbroken, armigerous, male line of descent from the early Middle Ages. Having survived the lean centuries, they celebrated the 'second Spring' of the nineteenth century and better times for their co-religionists by catching up architecturally with their Anglican neighbours.

Stephen Tempest VI married Elizabeth, co-heiress daughter of Henry Blundell, the sculpture collector. She brought to her husband a lucrative Lancashire estate with coal royalties and urban ground rents, which made the improvements possible, together with the complete refurnishing of the house by Gillow of Lancaster, whose most complete surviving ensemble it is. The Tempests also went on an extended Grand Tour in 1817 to buy art for their enlarged house, and had their portraits painted in Florence by the French Neo-Classical master F. X. Fabre.

William Atkinson enlarged the old house at Broughton in 1809–11, adding wings containing new drawing rooms and a breakfast room, and converting the old drawing room to a library. These rooms were further altered by George Webster for Elizabeth and Stephen's son,

Sir Charles Tempest, 1st Baronet. Webster remodelled the White Drawing Room with a new Carrara marble chimneypiece and sienna *scagliola* columns framing double doors to the Red Drawing Room, so that they could be opened up together for entertaining. Webster also brilliantly remodelled the exterior of the house. He refaced the old block in ashlar, adding a giant Ionic porte-cochère, and introduced the requisite Picturesque asymmetry with the subsidiary bedroom wing (screening the offices) culminating in the Grecian chapel bell turret, which helped to root the house into its beautiful landscape setting.

THE TRUBSHAWS OF STAFFORDSHIRE

Like the Websters, the Trubshaws were a family of builders and stonemasons who evolved into architects in the late-Georgian and

CHILLINGTON HALL, STAFFORDSHIRE Right: *The east front was designed by Sir John Soane in 1786, as his first major country house, but the interior was left unfinished and only fitted out in the 1820s in a heavy Grecian manner typical of the Trubshaws.*

Below: *The dining room. The plain marble chimneypiece and massive mahogany sideboard, with the Giffard panther crest on the doors, are characteristic of Regency dining rooms. The full-length portrait by Pompeo Batoni is of Soane's patron, Thomas Giffard.*

CHILLINGTON HALL, STAFFORDSHIRE Above: *The saloon. Soane had proposed a top-lit canopy dome for this large room, which occupies the site of the medieval Great Hall. Only the timber structure was executed, and the present stucco saucer dome with strongly modelled Grecian detail dates from the 1820s. The large antiquarian stone chimneypiece is a heraldic design which illustrates the Giffards' legendary panther crest.*

Left: *The entrance hall. The Grecian Ionic columns and cornice are almost identical to Trubshaw's work at Swynnerton Hall, another Catholic Staffordshire house, and – in the absence of surviving documentary evidence – this supports the attribution of the 1820s rooms at Chillington to James Trubshaw.*

Regency periods. James Trubshaw (1777–1853) was an engineer and architect, and a man of unusual physical strength. He once won a race against the chaplain at Ilam Hall, Staffordshire, carrying the sculptor Sir Francis Chantrey on his back. He was briefly with Richard Westmacott in London but on his father's death in 1808, he returned to Staffordshire to run the family business. Unlike the Wyatts, who started out in Staffordshire but moved to London, the Trubshaws stayed in the county for seven generations as architect-builders and had a reputation for absolute reliability, often executing work for other architects as well as designing themselves. One of James Trubshaw's major country house jobs was the interior remod-

elling of Swynnerton Hall, Staffordshire, for the Fitzherberts in 1810–11. His son, Thomas (1802–42), was also a competent country house architect.

Swynnerton has never been photographed by *Country Life*, but it is likely, by comparison, that Trubshaw was also responsible for the interior of Chillington Hall, Staffordshire, for the Giffards. Though there is a dearth of contemporary documentation (the Chillington archive was burnt in 1905), the slightly heavy Grecian character of the rooms at Chillington is similar to that of Swynnerton, and the Giffards were at that time one of the closely-knit Catholic recusant squirearchy, like their county neighbours, the Fitzherberts.

Chillington Hall had been largely rebuilt for Thomas Giffard by Sir John Soane in 1786. Soane kept the south wing, by Francis Smith of Warwick, but replaced the old house with a new front range dominated by a giant Ionic portico. The interior was only fitted up in the 1820s. This work included the hall, drawing room and dining room, with their simple cornices and chimneypieces, and the domed stucco ceiling and strange heraldic stone chimneypiece of the saloon. It is these rooms that are now attributed to James Trubshaw.

⇒ THE COTTAGE RESIDENCE ⇐

The fashion for the 'cottage' in the late eighteenth century was an aspect of the sentimentalisation of rural life at that time, as well as a love of English landscape and an architectural interest in 'primitive' simplicity. At first, genteel thatched cottages were usually ladies' dairies, as in Soane's 'primitive' designs for Bentley Priory and elsewhere, or other ornamental retreats and garden buildings, as well as model tenants' housing like Nash's Blaise Hamlet (1803). The idea of a 'cottage' as the main house of a gentleman, or even the subsidiary residence of a royal prince or nobleman, is a specifically Regency phenomenon and one made fashionable by the Prince Regent's Royal Lodge (1812), designed by Nash in Windsor Great Park. Though called a cottage, because it was thatched, Lord Brougham noted that the Royal Lodge was big enough to serve as 'a very comfortable residence for a family'. The Prince Regent put the seal of fashion on the genre, but he was not a pioneer in this field.

The earliest gentleman's house designed as a cottage was Houghton Lodge, overlooking the River Test in Hampshire. This was built *circa* 1800 and was probably the work of an amateur, because much of the interior Gothick detail derives from old-fashioned Batty Langley pattern books. The earliest major cottage residence was Endsleigh in Devon, designed by Wyatville for the 6th Duke of Bedford in 1810, at least partly at the instigation of the Duke's second wife, a Gordon, who was used to the Scottish tradition of Highland lodges in the glens around her ancestral castle. Others soon followed. Angeston Grange in Gloucestershire is almost a copy of Endsleigh and was designed as his main residence for a Stroud mill owner. The Websters of Kendal, for instance, when they set up as landed gentry themselves (on the strength of the money earned from the marble works, slate quarry and building construction, rather than the poorer rewards of architectural design), created their new seat at Eller Howe in the Lake District as a cottage residence.

HOUGHTON LODGE, STOCKBRIDGE, HAMPSHIRE Above: *This was the earliest Regency 'cottage residence' and was intended as a fishing lodge. It was probably designed by an amateur architect. The iron verandah was a good Victorian addition, as was the tiling of the roof which originally was thatched.*

Right: *The Picturesque view from the verandah to the River Test.*

HOUGHTON LODGE, HAMPSHIRE

This charming house with steep pitched roof (now tiled, but originally thatched), tall barley-sugar chimneys, pointed windows and prominent bow is almost undocumented. The only contemporary evidence is an advertisement for sale in *The Times* on 17 January 1801, which implied that it had been recently built, and extolled its merits: 'A singularly beautiful FREEHOLD COTTAGE, seated in a paddock of 30 acres ... commanding picturesque views of the River Test ...

HOUGHTON LODGE, STOCKBRIDGE, HAMPSHIRE Above: *The ceiling of the circular room. The domed ceiling retains original decoration and is painted as a sky with clouds and the ribs treated as ropes.* (Right): *The circular room was originally the dining room and the principal room of the house, rising the full height inside the bow. The ogival chimneypiece of white marble and bluejohn is derived from a Batty Langley engraving. The pointed glasses with coloured edges are highly unusual at this date.*

Left: *The drawing room with over-scaled trefoil arches, which are the architectural feature of the interior.*

The Cottage contains six bed-chambers and dressing rooms, a lofty elegant dining room ... finished in the highest style of Gothic architecture.'

Christopher Hussey attributed the house to Nash or Repton in his article on the place in *Country Life* in April 1951. It seems much more likely to have been designed by the owner, a member of the Bernard family on whose property it was built. In the early nineteenth century, it was let to Caleb Smith and then Mr George Pitt (later Lord Rivers) and was used as a lodge in connection with the trout fishing on the River Test.

ENDSLEIGH COTTAGE, DEVON

This unusually lavish 'cottage' is an important landmark in the evolution of the Picturesque ideal, and illustrates the increasing dominance of landscape over architecture in that the site was chosen (by the Duchess of Bedford) before the architect (Jeffry Wyatville) was appointed. The irregular plan and composition respects the setting and reflects the wish to keep the character of an ancient rustic farmhouse, 'an object so picturesque that it was impossible to wish it

ENDSLEIGH COTTAGE, DEVON Top: *Verandahs of trellis and tree trunks frame the views along the river valley.*

Above: *The sublime setting was enhanced by Repton's landscaping.*

removed and replaced by any other style of building', to quote
Repton, who was the landscape designer at Endsleigh. The foundation stone was laid by the Duchess and the four oldest Russell boys
on 7 September 1810. It proclaims the importance of 'this landscape
embosomed in all the sublimity of umbrageous majesty'.

The Duchess was the moving spirit behind Endsleigh. She was the
youngest daughter of the 4th Duke of Gordon of Gordon Castle in
the Highlands, and John Cornforth suggested that the inspiration for
Endsleigh was Scottish, and came from the lodges at Kinrara and
Glenfiddich on the Gordon estates. This was Repton and Wyatville's
second collaboration; they had previously worked together at
Longleat. The Endsleigh landscape is Repton's masterpiece, with its
scenic terrace, the Swiss Cottage, dairy, rustic seat and other ornamental features. Work continued from 1810 to 1818, and the whole
cost nearly £50,000. The main part of the house was finished by 1816
when the family paid their first visit for the summer.

Wyatville's bat's wing plan follows the contour – following Uvedale
Price's advice to accommodate the building to the scenery. It is
broken into three sections with the main rooms in the centre, the

eleven servants and domestic offices on one side and the twelve
children in their own semi-detached cottage on the other; the three
sections being linked by tree-trunk or trellis verandahs with paving of
deer knuckle bones and twig furniture. The layout and overall
composition shows Wyatville's gift for grouping and handling masses,
and his cleverness at planning houses, but also his insensitivity to
materials and textures. Repton wrote equivocally of the 'raw tints of
new materials', and the exterior needs all the smothering of creepers
to maintain its romantic appeal.

Endsleigh was designed very much as a retreat for family holidays,
and there was more provision for the children than for guests, with a
playroom, school room and a special children's garden (overlooked by
the Duchess's sitting room). There were only four guest rooms, as the
Russells did all their princely entertaining at Woburn and escaped to
Endsleigh in the summer, where the Duchess could mother her clever
brood, described by Lady Holland as 'a better race than Atridae …
the best tribe that we have', and the Duke could pursue his botanical
interests. As he said himself: 'Gardening is my hobbyhorse and chief
occupation and amusement'; the grounds at Endsleigh were filled

ENDSLEIGH COTTAGE, DEVON Top: *The dining room. The wall panelling retains the original decoration, with Gothic tracery and heraldry. The sideboard and chairs were designed by Wyatville; only the former has been left in situ as a fixture. The chimneypiece is of Dartmoor granite, typical of the Regency interest in local stones.*

Above: *The library. The 6th Duke's botanical books have been removed to Woburn. The little plaster casts of Roman statues were acquired by the Bedfords on their foreign tour in 1815 and sold in 2004.*

with rare trees and shrubs and the library with his splendid colour plate botanical books.

Endsleigh was designed for this happy and relaxed family life with the Duke and Duchess's day rooms, the book room, sitting parlour and dining room. The interior was oak grained, with some heraldry and oak furniture designed by Wyatville. As J. P. Neale put it: 'The furniture corresponds in all respects with the exquisite simplicity of the habitation.' The house continued as a holiday home of the Russells down to the 1950s, when it was sold with many of the original contents to a fishing club, which maintained it well. The setting up of a charitable trust in the 1990s in association with the Heritage Lottery Fund, however, proved a disastrous failure and most of the integral contents were sold by Christie's in 2004, with no official effort to save them. The place is now being converted into a hotel. The black-and-white photographs record the house as it was when in family occupation; and the colour photographs, taken as

recently as 1997, under the benevolent regime of the fishing club, show it before the regrettable sale of the historic contents.

ANGESTON GRANGE, GLOUCESTERSHIRE

This almost unknown house resembles a smaller version of Endsleigh. It was built as his main residence by Nathaniel Lloyd, a clothing manufacturer, *circa* 1811, in a romantic setting in the Uley valley near Stroud. Lloyd made a fortune from cloth for military uniforms during the Napoleonic Wars but went bankrupt in 1826 and was forced to sell his new house. No designer is known, but it has been attributed to J. A. Repton, the architect son of Humphry Repton, who would have known of Endsleigh through his father's collaboration with Wyatville. The original room uses are recorded in the 1826 sales particulars and included the Regency stalwarts: library, billiard room and dining room. The staircase is octagonal. The canted plan, as at Endsleigh, follows the contour of the hillside. The ochre-washed stucco, ornamental bargeboards and barley-sugar chimneys make a delightful foil to the oak trees in which it nestles. Angeston is a successful combination of the Picturesque and the mercantile, and demonstrates the wide appeal of the cottage residence.

ANGESTON GRANGE, GLOUCESTERSHIRE Above: *This large, Romantically sited cottage orné was built c. 1811 by Nathaniel Lloyd, a clothing manufacturer who had made a fortune from military uniforms in the Wars. The design is attributed to J. A. Repton.*

Thomas Hope (1769–1831), the Scottish-Dutch banker, bought his famous house in Duchess Street, London, in 1799, arranged his collections of Greek vases and antique and Neo-Classical sculpture there, and set about improving English taste and promoting the Greek Revival. A shrewd self-publicist, he opened Duchess Street to the public in 1804, and in 1806 published *Household Furniture*, with engravings of his own designs and interiors, combining the influence of Percier & Fontaine in Paris and extreme archaeological derivations. The following year he got married to Louisa Beresford and acquired The Deepdene estate in Surrey from the Burrells, to whom the 11th Duke of Norfolk had sold this former Howard property in 1791.

Through his writings and example and campaigning, Hope had a large influence on the forms and style of contemporary Regency decoration and furniture, and helped to disseminate Neo-Classical ideas among contemporary architects and decorators. The Deepdene was an important part of his aesthetic proselytising campaign. A series

of alterations, remodellings, extensions and improvements transformed the place into the ideal Picturesque Neo-Classical house, set in an Italianate landscape.

When Hope bought the property, the house was a boring red-brick villa designed and built by a London surveyor, William Gowan, for the future 10th Duke of Norfolk in 1769–75. The landscape, however, was the *locus classicus* of Italophile gardening in England. The 'Collector' Earl of Arundel had even introduced large edible Italian snails there in the seventeenth century (which still flourish) and

THE DEEPDENE, SURREY Right: *View down from the amphitheatre to the house; part of the Italian garden created by Charles Howard with John Evelyn's advice in the late seventeenth century and a feature which encouraged Thomas Hope to acquire the property in 1807. In the background can be seen Box Hill (with descendants of seventeenth-century edible Italian snails and box trees). Photographed in 1899.*

Below: *The drawing room in 1899. The form of the room with a bow window and apsidal inner wall survived from Gowan's villa. One of Hope's gilt lion monopodia tables is visible in the foreground. The characteristic white marble and ormolu chimneypiece and the large overmantel mirror with gilt lotus capitals are also his work.*

planted box trees in the vicinity. The Collector's grandson, Charles The Alchemist, a founder member of the Royal Society, had laid out an Italian garden with John Evelyn's advice after the Restoration, incorporating an amphitheatre and grotto which survived in the early nineteenth century, while the views towards Box Hill with its evergreens, and other wooded Surrey eminences, were the epitome of English Classical landscape taste. The setting was Thomas Hope's inspiration and he set about enhancing the Italianate quality with architectural appendages, formal terraces, statues, rare shrubs and pots of exotic plants.

The house, too, was transformed in phases. Hope, himself an amateur architect, employed William Atkinson (1773–1839) to execute his own ideas and abolish Gowan's stilted symmetries. In 1818–19, they added two side wings, a new entrance front, offices and stables and a Picturesque tower. The following year the external brickwork was stuccoed. In 1823, an entirely new asymmetrical range was added at an oblique angle, containing such quintessential Regency amenities as a conservatory and sculpture gallery. J. P. Neale, the topographer, noted in 1826 that the former red-brick villa had by then been transformed into 'a spacious mansion of pleasing colour, diversified and varied in its features'. As David Watkin has written, the result was 'a perfect epitome of Regency taste' in its asymmetry and eclectic archaeological Classicism with Greek, Egyptian, French, Italianate and castellated styles rubbing shoulders.

Neale described the richly magnificent interior as it was in Hope's lifetime. The entrance hall had marble walls, four antique Corinthian columns and statuary, including a copy of Canova's *Venus*. The staircase had a bronze palmette balustrade, while the first-floor landing was supported by a Greek *canephora*. The drawing room behind Gowan's central bay window was hung with blue satin, the chimneypiece embellished with ormolu mounts and crowned with a large tripartite looking glass framed by gilt colonnettes with lotus capitals. The boudoir had a green Mona marble chimneypiece with ormolu lotus capitals and a tent bed surmounted by swans. The libraries had bas reliefs, gilt stencilled doors and ormolu-mounted chimneypieces. The Egyptian bedroom contained a bed made after the model illustrated in Denon's *Egypte* (1802).

After Hope's death, the house was further remodelled in the 1830s and 1840s by his son, Henry Thomas Hope, who rebuilt the entrance front with twin towers, created a new large peristyle hall, and generally transformed the place into a High Renaissance *palazzo*. After his death, the house was let out. When photographed (but not published) by *Country Life* in 1899, it was occupied by Lord William Beresford. Hope's collections and decoration were still intact, but Beresford overlaid them with his own gleanings from the East and big-game trophies to create an effect of supreme incongruity, tiger

THE DEEPDENE, SURREY *The Vase Room in 1899. Thomas Hope's famous collection of Greek vases survived in its original arrangement. The magnificent ormolu chandelier shows the influence of Percier & Fontaine. Amid Beresford's exotic tat can be seen Hope's most famous set of Grecian chairs (now at Buscot Park).*

skins and trashy Indian coffee tables jostling amphoras, Klismos
chairs, and Thorwaldsen and Canova sculptures.

And here began the Regency Revival. The further history of
The Deepdene, culminating in demolition by British Rail in 1967, is
depressing in the extreme, and a veil will be drawn over that. But out
of the ruin and despoliation of Hope's life's work arose the twentieth-
century Regency Revival. At the sale of the Hope Heirlooms by
Christie's in 1917, the Anglo-American collector-aesthete Edward
Knoblock bought many of the best pieces of furniture, while the
Greek vases and sculptures went to the Lady Lever Art Gallery, and
Hope's Thorwaldsens (including his own bust) to the sculptor's
eponymous museum in Copenhagen.

Knoblock acquired The Beach House, Worthing, on the Sussex
coast and transformed that plain early-nineteenth-century villa into
the first twentieth-century Regency Revival country house, in collaboration with his architect Maxwell Ayrton. Published by Christopher
Hussey in a pioneering article in *Country Life* in 1921, the photographs show Hope's collection redeployed in a modern Thomas Hope
interior which has remained an influential architectural inspiration
ever since.

THE BEACH HOUSE, SUSSEX Top: *The drawing room in 1921.
On the walls are panels of French Napoleonic period* papier peint, *in
stencilled Grecian frames.*

Above: *An alcoved bedroom with Regency furniture.*

Left: *The interior designed by Maxwell Ayrton sported all the hallmarks
of the Regency Revival style: marbled walls, Egyptian chimneypiece,
Colza oil ormolu chandelier and Grecian furniture.*

INDEX